# FAST IN THE ICE,

## ADVENTURES IN THE POLAR REGIONS

## R. M. BALLANTYNE

1st WORLD
LIBRARY
Literary Society

# Fast in the Ice

## R. M. Ballantyne

© 1st World Library, 2009
PO Box 2211
Fairfield, IA 52556
www.1stworldlibrary.com
First Edition

LCCN: 2009923488

Softcover ISBN: 978-1-4218-8875-0
Hardcover ISBN: 978-1-4218-8974-0
eBook ISBN: 978-1-4218-8776-0

Purchase *"Fast in the Ice"*
as a traditional bound book at:
www.1stWorldLibrary.com/purchase.asp?ISBN=978-1-4218-8875-0

# 1$^{st}$ World Library Literary Society

## Giving Back to the World

"If you want to work on the core problem, it's early school literacy."

**- James Barksdale, former CEO of Netscape**

"No skill is more crucial to the future of a child, or to a democratic and prosperous society, than literacy."

**- Los Angeles Times**

"Literacy... means far more than learning how to read and write... The aim is to transmit... knowledge and promote social participation."

**- UNESCO**

"Literacy is not a luxury, it is a right and a responsibility. If our world is to meet the challenges of the twenty-first century we must harness the energy and creativity of all our citizens."

**- President Bill Clinton**

"Parents should be encouraged to read to their children, and teachers should be equipped with all available techniques for teaching literacy, so the varying needs and capacities of individual kids can be taken into account."

**- Hugh Mackay**

# CHAPTER ONE

One day, many years ago, a brig cast off from her moorings, and sailed from a British port for the Polar Seas. That brig never came back.

Many a hearty cheer was given, many a kind wish was uttered, many a handkerchief was waved, and many a tearful eye gazed that day as the vessel left Old England, and steered her course into the unknown regions of the far north.

But no cheer ever greeted her return; no bright eyes ever watched her homeward-bound sails rising on the far-off horizon.

Battered by the storms of the Arctic seas, her sails and cordage stiffened by the frosts, and her hull rasped and shattered by the ice of those regions, she was forced on a shore where the green grass has little chance to grow, where winter reigns nearly all the year round, where man never sends his merchandise, and never drives his plough. There the brig was frozen in; there, for two long years, she lay unable to move, and her starving crew forsook her; there, year after year, she lay, unknown, unvisited by civilised man, and unless the wild Eskimos [see note 1] have torn her to pieces, and made spears of her timbers, or the ice has swept her out to sea and whirled her to destruction, there she lies still—hard and fast in the ice.

The vessel was lost, but her crew were saved, and most of them returned to tell their kinsfolk of the wonders and the dangers of the frozen regions, where God has created some of the most beautiful and some of the most awful objects that were ever looked on by the eye of man.

What was told by the fireside, long ago, is now recounted in this book.

Imagine a tall, strong man, of about five-and-forty, with short, curly black hair, just beginning to turn grey; stern black eyes, that look as if they could pierce into your secret thoughts; a firm mouth, with lines of good-will and kindness lurking about it; a deeply-browned skin, and a short, thick beard and moustache. That is a portrait of the commander of the brig. His name was Harvey. He stood on the deck, close by the wheel, looking wistfully over the stern. As the vessel bent before the breeze, and cut swiftly through the water, a female hand was raised among the gazers on the pier, and a white scarf waved in the breeze. In the forefront of the throng, and lower down, another hand was raised; it was a little one, but very vigorous; it whirled a cap round a small head of curly black hair, and a shrill "hurrah!" came floating out to sea.

The captain kissed his hand and waved his hat in reply; then, wheeling suddenly round, he shouted, in a voice of thunder:

"Mind your helm, there; let her away a point. Take a pull on these foretopsail halyards; look alive, lads!"

"Aye, aye, sir!" replied the men.

R. M. Ballantyne

There was no occasion whatever for these orders. The captain knew that well enough, but he had his own reasons for giving them. The men knew that, too, and they understood his reasons when they observed the increased sternness of his eyes, and the compression of his lips.

Inclination and duty! What wars go on in the hearts of men—high and low, rich and poor—between these two. What varied fortune follows man, according as the one or the other carries the day.

"Please, sir," said a gruff, broad-shouldered, and extremely short man, with little or no forehead, a hard, vacant face, and a pair of enormous red whispers; "please, sir, Sam Baker's took very bad; I think it would be as well if you could give him a little physic, sir; a tumbler of Epsom, or some-think of that sort."

"Why, Mr Dicey, there can't be anything very far wrong with Baker," said the captain, looking down at his second mate; "he seems to me one of the healthiest men in the ship. What's the matter with him?"

"Well, I can't say, sir," replied Mr Dicey, "but he looks 'orrible bad, all yellow and green about the gills, and fearful red round the eyes. But what frightens me most is that I heard him groanin' very heavy about a quarter of an hour ago, and then I saw him suddenly fling himself into his 'ammock and begin blubberin' like a child. Now, sir, I say, when a grow'd-up man gives way like that, there must be some-think far wrong with his inside. And it's a serious thing, sir, to take a sick man on such a voyage as this."

"Does he not say what's wrong with him?" asked the captain.

"No, sir; he don't. He says it's nothin', and he'll be all right if he's only let alone. I did hear him once or twice muttering some-think about his wife and child; you know, sir, he's got a young wife, and she had a baby about two months 'fore we came away, but I can't think that's got much to do with it, for *I've* got a wife myself, sir, and six children, two of 'em bein' babies, and that don't upset *me*, and Baker's a much stronger man."

"You are right, Mr Dicey, he is a much stronger man than you," replied the captain, "and I doubt not that his strength will enable him to get over this without the aid of physic."

"Very well, sir," said Mr Dicey.

The second mate was a man whose countenance never showed any signs of emotion, no matter what he felt. He seldom laughed, or, if he did, his mouth remained almost motionless, and the sounds that came out were anything but cheerful. He had light grey eyes which always wore an expression of astonishment; but the expression was accidental; it indicated no feeling. He would have said, "Very well, sir," if the captain had refused to give poor Baker food instead of physic.

"And hark'ee, Mr Dicey," said the captain, "don't let him be disturbed till he feels inclined to move."

"Very well, sir," replied the second mate, touching his cap as he turned away.

"So," murmured the captain, as he gazed earnestly at the now distant shore, "I'm not the only one who carries a heavy heart to sea this day and leaves sorrowing hearts behind him."

Note 1. This word is here spelled as pronounced. It is usually spelled Esquimaux.

# CHAPTER TWO

## AT SEA—THE FIRST STORM

It is now hundreds of years since the North polar regions began to attract general attention. Men have long felt very inquisitive about that part of the earth, and many good ships, many noble lives have been lost in trying to force a passage through the ice that encumbers the Arctic seas, summer and winter. Britain has done more than other nations in the cause of discovery within the Arctic circle. The last and greatest of her Arctic heroes perished there— the famous Sir John Franklin.

Were I writing a history of those regions I would have much to say of other countries as well as of our own. But such is not my object in this book. I mean simply to follow in the wake of one of Britain's adventurous discoverers, and thus give the reader an idea of the fortunes of those gallant men who risk life and limb for the sake of obtaining knowledge of distant lands.

There have always been restless spirits in this country. There have ever been men who, when boys, were full of mischief, and who could "settle to nothing" when they grew up. Lucky for us, lucky for the world, that such is the case! Many of our "restless spirits," as we call them,

R. M. Ballantyne

have turned out to be our heroes, our discoverers, our greatest men. No doubt many of them have become our drones, our sharpers, our blacklegs. But that is just saying that some men are good, while others are bad—no blame is due to what is called the restlessness of spirit. Our restless men, if good, find rest in action; in bold energetic toil; if bad, they find rest, alas! in untimely graves.

Captain Harvey was one of our restless spirits. He had a deeply learned friend who said to him one day that he felt sure "*there was a sea of open water round the North Pole!*" Hundreds of ships had tried to reach that pole without success, because they always found a barrier of thick ice raised against them. This friend said that if a ship could only cut or force its way through the ice to a certain latitude north, open water would be found. Captain Harvey was much interested in this. He could not rest until he had proved it. He had plenty of money, so had his friend. They resolved to buy a vessel and send it to the seas lying within the Arctic circle. Other rich friends helped them; a brig was bought, it was named the *Hope*, and, as we have seen in the last chapter, it finally set sail under command of Captain Harvey.

Many days and nights passed, and the *Hope* kept her course steadily toward the coast of North America. Greenland was the first land they hoped to see. Baffin's Bay was the strait through which they hoped to reach the open polar sea.

The *Hope* left England as a whaler, with all the boats, lances, harpoons, lines, and other apparatus used in the whale fishery. It was intended that she should do a little business in that way if Captain Harvey thought it advisable, but the discovery of new lands and seas was their chief end and aim.

At first the weather was fine, the wind fair, and the voyage prosperous. But one night there came a deep calm. Not a breath of air moved over the sea, which was as clear and polished as a looking-glass. The captain walked the deck with the surgeon of the ship, a nephew of his own, named Gregory.

Tom Gregory was a youth of about nineteen, who had not passed through the whole course of a doctor's education, but who was a clever fellow, and better able to cut and carve and physic poor suffering humanity than many an older man who wrote M.D. after his name. He was a fine, handsome, strapping fellow, with a determined manner and a kind heart. He was able to pull an oar with the best man aboard, and could even steer the brig in fine weather, if need be. He was hearty and romantic, and a great favourite with the men. He, too, was a restless spirit. He had grown tired of college life, and had made up his mind to take a year's run into the Polar regions, by way of improving his knowledge of the "outlandish" parts of the world.

"I don't like the look of the sky to-day, Tom," said the captain, glancing at the horizon and then at the sails.

"Indeed!" said Tom, in surprise. "It seems to me the most beautiful afternoon we have had since the voyage began. But I suppose you seamen are learned in signs which we landsmen do not understand."

"Perhaps we are," replied the captain; "but it does not require much knowledge of the weather to say that such a dead calm as this, and such unusual heat, is not likely to end in a gentle breeze."

"You don't object to a stiff breeze, uncle?" said the youth.

R. M. Ballantyne

"No, Tom; but I don't like a storm, because it does us no good, and may do us harm."

"Storms do you no good, uncle!" cried Tom; "how can you say so? Why, what is it that makes our sailors such trumps? The British tar would not be able to face danger as he does if there were no storms."

"True, Tom, but the British tar would not require to face danger at all if there were no storms. What says the barometer, Mr Mansell?' said the captain, looking down the skylight into the cabin, where the first mate—a middle-sized man of thirty-five, or thereabouts—was seated at the table writing up the ship's log-book.

"The glass has gone down an inch, sir, and is still falling," answered the mate.

"Reef the topsail, Mr Dicey," cried the captain, on hearing this.

"Why such haste?" inquired Gregory.

"Because such a sudden fall in the barometer is a sure sign of approaching bad weather," answered the captain.

The first man on the shrouds and out upon the main-topsail yard was Sam Baker, whose active movements and hearty manner showed that he had quite recovered his health without the use of physic. He was quickly followed by some of his shipmates, all of whom were picked men—able in body and ready for anything.

In a few minutes sail was reduced. Soon after that clouds began to rise on the horizon and spread over the sky. Before half an hour had passed the breeze came—came far stronger than had been expected—and the order to take in sail had to be repeated. Baker was first again. He was closely followed by Joe Davis and Jim Croft, both of them sturdy fellows—good specimens of the British seaman. Davy Butts, who came next, was not so good a specimen. He was nearly six feet high, very thin and loosely put together, like a piece of bad furniture. But his bones were big, and he was stronger than he looked. He would not have formed one of such a crew had he not been a good man. The rest of the crew, of whom there were eighteen, not including the officers, were of all shapes, sizes, and complexions.

The sails had scarcely been taken in when the storm burst on the brig in all its fury. The waves rose like mountains and followed after her, as if they were eager to swallow her up. The sky grew dark overhead as the night closed in, the wind shrieked through the rigging, and the rag of canvas that they ventured to hoist seemed about to burst away from the yard. It was an awful night. Such a night as causes even reckless men to feel how helpless they are— how dependent on the arm of God. The gale steadily increased until near midnight, when it blew a perfect hurricane.

"It's a dirty night," observed the captain, to the second mate, as the latter came on deck to relieve the watch.

"It is, sir," replied Mr Dicey, as coolly as if he were about to sit down to a good dinner on shore. Mr Dicey was a remarkably matter-of-fact man. He looked upon a storm as he looked upon a fit of the toothache—a thing that had to be endured, and was not worth making a fuss about.

"It won't last long," said the captain.

R. M. Ballantyne

"No, sir; it won't," answered Mr Dicey.

As Mr Dicey did not seem inclined to say more, the captain went below and flung himself on a locker, having given orders that he should be called if any change for the worse took place in the weather. Soon afterward a tremendous sea rose high over the stern, and part of it fell on the deck with a terrible crash, washing Mr Dicey into the lee-scuppers, and almost sweeping him overboard. On regaining his feet, and his position beside the wheel, the second mate shook himself and considered whether he ought to call the captain. Having meditated some time, he concluded that the weather was no worse, although it had treated him very roughly, so he did not disturb the captain's repose.

Thus the storm raged all that night. It tossed the *Hope* about like a cork; it well-nigh blew the sails off the masts, and almost blew Mr Dicey's head off his shoulders! then it stopped as it had begun—suddenly.

## CHAPTER THREE

## IN THE ICE—DANGERS OF ARCTIC VOYAGING

Next morning the *Hope* was becalmed in the midst of a scene more beautiful than the tongue or the pen of man can describe.

When the sun rose that day, it shone upon what appeared to be a field of glass and a city of crystal. Every trace of the recent storm was gone except a long swell, which caused the brig to roll considerably, but which did not break the surface of the sea.

Ice was to be seen all round as far as the eye could reach. Ice in every form and size imaginable. And the wonderful thing about it was that many of the masses resembled the buildings of a city. There were houses, and churches, and monuments, and spires, and ruins. There were also islands and mountains! Some of the pieces were low and flat, no bigger than a boat; others were tall, with jagged tops; some of the fields, as they are called, were a mile and more in extent, and there were a number of bergs, or ice-mountains, higher than the brig's topmasts. These last were almost white, but they had, in many places, a greenish-blue colour that was soft and beautiful. The whole scene shone and sparkled so brilliantly in the

R. M. Ballantyne

morning sun, that one could almost fancy it was one of the regions of fairyland!

When young Gregory came on the quarter-deck, no one was there except Jim Croft, a short, thick-set man, with the legs of a dwarf and the shoulders of a giant. He stood at the helm, and although no steering was required, as there was no wind, he kept his hands on the spokes of the wheel, and glanced occasionally at the compass. The first mate, who had the watch on deck, was up at the masthead, observing the state of the ice.

"How glorious!" exclaimed the youth, as he swept his sparkling eye round the horizon. "Ah, Croft! is not this splendid?"

"So it is, sir," said the seaman, turning the large quid of tobacco that bulged out his left cheek. "It's very beautiful, no doubt, but it's comin' rather thick for my taste."

"How so?" inquired Gregory. "There seems to me plenty of open water to enable us to steer clear of these masses. Besides, as we have no wind, it matters little, I should think, whether we have room to sail or not."

"You've not seed much o' the ice yet, that's plain," said Croft, "else you'd know that the floes are closin' round us, an' we'll soon be fast in the pack, if a breeze don't spring up to help us."

As the reader may not, perhaps, understand the terms used by Arctic voyagers in regard to the ice in its various forms, it may be as well here to explain the meaning of those most commonly used.

When ice is seen floating in small detached pieces and

scattered masses, it is called "floe" ice, and men speak of getting among the floes. When these floes close up, so that the whole sea seems to be covered with them, and little water can be seen, it is called "pack" ice. When the pack is squeezed together, so that lumps of it are forced up in the form of rugged mounds, these mounds are called "hummocks." A large mass of flat ice, varying from one mile to many miles in extent, is called a "field," and a mountain of ice is called a "berg."

All the ice here spoken of, except the berg, is sea-ice; formed by the freezing of the ocean in winter. The berg is formed in a very different manner. Of this more shall be said in a future chapter.

"Well, my lad," said Gregory, in reply to Jim Croft's last observation, "I have not seen much of the ice yet, as you truly remark, so I hope that the wind will not come to help us out of it for some time. You don't think it dangerous to get into the pack, do you?"

"Well, not exactly dangerous, sir," replied Croft, "but I must say that it aint safe, 'specially when there's a swell on like this. But that'll go down soon. D'ye know what a nip is, Dr Gregory?"

"I think I do; at least I have read of such a thing. But I should be very glad to hear what you have to say about it. No doubt you have felt one."

"Felt one!" cried Jim, screwing up his face and drawing his limbs together, as if he were suffering horrible pain, "no, I've never felt one. The man what *feels* a nip aint likely to live to tell what his feelin's was. But I've *seed* one."

R. M. Ballantyne

"You've seen one, have you? That must have been interesting. Where was it?"

"Not very far from the Greenland coast," said Croft, giving his quid another turn. "This was the way of it. You must know that there was two ships of us in company at the time. Whalers we was. We got into the heart of the pack somehow, and we thought we'd never get out of it again. There was nothin' but ice all round us as far as the eye could see. The name of our ship was the *Nancy*. Our comrade was the *Bullfinch*. One mornin' early we heard a loud noise of ice rubbin' agin the sides o' the ship, so we all jumped up, an' on deck as fast as we could, for there's short time given to save ourselves in them seas sometimes. The whole pack, we found, was in motion, and a wide lead of water opened up before us, for all the world like a smooth river or canal windin' through the pack. Into this we warped the ship, and hoistin' sail, steered away cheerily. We passed close to the *Bullfinch*, which was still hard and fast in the pack, and we saw that her crew were sawin' and cuttin' away at the ice, tryin' to get into the lead that we'd got into. So we hailed them, and said we would wait for 'em outside the pack, if we got through. But the words were no sooner spoken, when the wind it died away, and we were becalmed about half a mile from the *Bullfinch*.

"'You'd better go down to breakfast, boys,' says our captain, says he, 'the breeze won't be long o' comin' again.'"

"So down the men went, and soon after that the steward comes on deck, and, says he to the captain, 'Breakfast, sir.' 'Very good,' says the captain, and down he went too, leavin' me at the wheel and the mate in charge of the deck. He'd not been gone three minutes when I noticed that the great field of ice on our right was closin' in on the field on our left, and the channel we was floatin' in was closin' up. The mate noticed it, too, but he wouldn't call the captain 'cause the ice came so slowly and quietly on that for a few minutes we could hardly believe it was movin' and everything around us looked so calm and peaceful like that it was difficult to believe our danger was so great. But this was only a momentary feelin', d'ye see. A minute after that the mate he cries down to the captain:—

"'Ice closin' up, sir!'

"And the captain he runs on deck. By this time there was no mistake about it; the ice was close upon us. It was clear that we were to have a nip. So the captain roars down the hatchway, 'Tumble up there! tumble up! every man alive! for your lives!' And sure enough they did tumble up, as I never seed 'em do it before—two or three of 'em was sick; they came up with their clothes in their hands. The ice was now almost touchin' our sides, and I tell *you*, sir, I never did feel so queerish in all my life before as when I looked over the side at the edge of that great field of ice which rose three foot out o' the water, and was, I suppose, six foot more below the surface. It came on so slow that we could hardly see the motion. Inch by inch the water narrowed between it and our sides. At last it touched on the left side, and that shoved us quicker on to the field on our right. Every eye was fixed on it—every man held his breath. You might have heard a pin fall on the deck. It touched gently at first, then there was a low grindin' and crunchin' sound. The ship trembled as if it had been a livin' creetur, and the beams began to crack. Now, you must know, sir, that when a nip o' this sort takes a ship the ice usually eases off, after giving her a good squeeze, or when the pressure is too much for her,

R. M. Ballantyne

the ice slips under her bottom and lifts her right out o' the water. But our *Nancy* was what we call wall-sided. She was never fit to sail in them seas. The consequence was that the ice crushed her sides in. The moment the captain heard the beams begin to go he knew it was all up with the ship; so he roared to take to the ice for our lives! You may be sure we took his advice. Over the side we went, every man Jack of us, and got on the ice. We did not take time to save an article belongin' to us; and it was as well we did not, for the ice closed up with a crash, and we heard the beams and timbers rending like a fire of musketry in the hold. Her bottom must have been cut clean away, for she stood on the ice just as she had floated on the sea. Then the noise stopped, the ice eased off, and the ship began to settle. The lead of water opened up again; in ten minutes after that the *Nancy* went to the bottom and left us standing there on the ice.

"It was the mercy of God that let it happen so near the *Bullfinch*. We might have been out o' sight o' that ship at the time, and then every man of us would have bin lost. As it was, we had a hard scramble over a good deal of loose ice, jumpin' from lump to lump, and some of us fallin' into the water several times, before we got aboard. Now that was a bad nip, sir, warn't it?"

"It certainly was," replied Gregory; "and although I delight in being among the ice, I sincerely hope that our tight little brig may not be tried in the same way. But she is better able to stand it, I should think."

"That she is, sir," replied Croft, with much confidence. "I seed her in dock, sir, when they was a-puttin' of extra timbers on the bow, and I do believe she would stand twice as much bad usage as the *Nancy* got, though she is only half the size."

Jim Croft's opinion on this point was well founded, for the *Hope* had indeed been strengthened and prepared for her ice battles with the greatest care, by men of experience and ability. As some readers may be interested in this subject, I shall give a brief account of the additions that were made to her hull.

The vessel was nearly two hundred tons burden. She had originally been built very strongly, and might even have ventured on a voyage to the Polar seas just as she was. But Captain Harvey resolved to take every precaution to insure the success of his voyage, and the safety and comfort of his men. He, therefore, had the whole of the ship's bottom sheathed with thick hardwood planking, which was carried up above her water-line, as high as the ordinary floe-ice would be likely to reach. The hull inside was strengthened with stout cross-beams, as well as with beams running along the length of the vessel, and in every part that was likely to be subjected to pressure iron stanchions were fastened. But the bow of the vessel was the point where the utmost strength was aimed at. Inside, just behind the cutwater, the whole space was so traversed by cross-beams of oak that it almost became a solid mass, and outside the sharp stem was cased in iron so as to resemble a giant's chisel. The false keel was taken off, the whole vessel, in short, was rendered as strong, outside and in, as wood and iron and skill could make her. It need scarcely be said that all the other arrangements about her were made with the greatest care and without regard to expense, for although the owners of the brig did not wish to waste their money, they set too high a value on human life to risk it for the sake of saving a few pounds. She was provisioned for a cruise of two years and a half. But this was in case of accidents, for Captain Harvey did not intend to be absent much longer than one year.

R. M. Ballantyne

But, to return to our story:

Jim Croft's fear that they would be set fast was realised sooner than he expected. The floes began to close in, from no cause that could be seen, for the wind was quite still, and in a short time the loose ice pressed against the *Hope* on all sides. It seemed to young Gregory as if the story that the seaman had just related was about to be enacted over again; and, being a stranger to ice, he could not help feeling a little uneasy for some time. But there was in reality little or no danger, for the pressure was light, and the brig had got into a small bay in the edge of an ice-field, which lay in the midst of the smaller masses.

Seeing that there was little prospect of the pack opening up just then, the captain ordered the ice-anchors to be got out and fixed.

The appearance of the sea from the brig's deck was now extremely wintry, but very bright and cheerful. Not a spot of blue water was to be seen in any direction. The whole ocean appeared as if it had been frozen over.

It was now past noon, and the sun's rays were warm, although the quantity of ice around rendered the air cold. As the men were returning from fixing the anchors, the captain looked over the side, and said:

"It's not likely that we shall move out of this for some hours. What say you, lads, to a game of football?"

The proposal was received with a loud cheer. The ball had been prepared by the sail-maker, in expectation of some such opportunity as this. It was at once tossed over the side; those men who were not already on the field scrambled out of the brig, and the entire crew went leaping and yelling over the ice with the wild delight of schoolboys let loose for an unexpected holiday.

They were in the middle of the game when a loud shout came from the brig, and the captain's voice was heard singing out:

"All hands ahoy! come aboard. Look alive!"

Instantly the men turned, and there was a general race toward the brig, which lay nearly a quarter of a mile distant from them.

In summer, changes in the motions of the ice take place in the most unexpected manner. Currents in the ocean are, no doubt, the chief cause of these; the action of winds has also something to do with them. One of these changes was now taking place. Almost before the men got on board the ice had separated, and long canals of water were seen opening up here and there. Soon after that a light breeze sprang up, the ice-anchors were taken aboard, the sails trimmed, and soon the *Hope* was again making her way slowly but steadily to the north.

R. M. Ballantyne

# CHAPTER FOUR

## DIFFICULTIES, TROUBLES, AND DANGERS

For some hours the brig proceeded onward with a freshening breeze, winding and turning in order to avoid the lumps of ice. Many of the smaller pieces were not worth turning out of the way of, the mere weight of the vessel being sufficient to push them aside.

Up to this time they had succeeded in steering clear of everything without getting a thump; but they got one at last, which astonished those among the crew who had not been in the ice before. The captain, Gregory, and Dicey were seated in the cabin at the time taking tea. Ned Dawkins, the steward, an active little man, was bringing in a tea-pot with a second supply of tea. In his left hand he carried a tray of biscuit. The captain sat at the head of the table, Dicey at the foot, and the doctor at the side.

Suddenly a tremendous shock was felt! The captain's cup of tea leaped away from him and flooded the centre of the table. The doctor's cup was empty; he seized the table with both hands and remained steady; but Dicey's cup happened to be at his lips at the moment, and was quite full. The effect on him was unfortunate. He was thrown violently on his back, and the tea poured over his face and drenched his hair as he lay sprawling on the floor. The steward saved himself by dropping the bread-tray and grasping the handle of the cabin door. So violent was the shock that the ship's bell was set a-ringing.

"Beg pardon, gentlemen," cried the first mate, looking down the skylight. "I forgot to warn you. The ice is getting rather thick around us, and I had to charge a lump of it."

"It's all very well to beg pardon," said the captain, "but that won't mend my crockery!"

"Or dry my head," growled Mr Dicey; "it's as bad as if I'd been dipped overboard, it is."

Before Mr Dicey's grumbling remarks were finished all three of them had reached the deck. The wind had freshened considerably, and the brig was rushing in a somewhat alarming manner among the floes. It required the most careful attention to prevent her striking heavily.

"If it goes on like this, we shall have to reduce sail," observed the captain. "See, there is a neck of ice ahead that will stop us."

This seemed to be probable, for the lane of water along which they were steering was, just ahead of them, stopped by a neck of ice that connected two floe-pieces. The water beyond was pretty free from ice, but this neck or mass seemed so thick that it became a question whether they should venture to charge it or shorten sail.

"Stand by the fore-and main-topsail braces!" shouted the captain.

R. M. Ballantyne

"Aye, aye, sir!"

"Now, Mr Mansell," said he, with a smile, "we have come to our first real difficulty. What do you advise; shall we back the topsails, or try what our little *Hope* is made of, and charge the enemy?"

"Charge!" answered the mate.

"Just so," said the captain, hastening to the bow to direct the steersman. "Port your helm."

"Steady."

The brig was now about fifty yards from the neck of ice, tearing through the water like a race-horse. In another moment she was up to it and struck it fair in the middle. The stout little vessel quivered to her keel under the shock, but she did not recoil. She split the mass into fragments, and, bearing down all before her, sailed like a conqueror into the clear water beyond.

"Well done the *Hope*!" said the captain, as he walked aft, while a cheer burst from the men.

"I think she ought to be called the *Good Hope* ever after this," said Tom Gregory. "If she cuts her way through everything as easily as she has cut through that neck of ice, we shall reach the North Pole itself before winter."

"If we reach the North Pole *at all*," observed Mr Dicey, "I'll climb up to the top of it and stand on my head, I will!"

The second mate evidently had no expectation of reaching that mysterious pole, which men have so long and so often tried to find, in vain.

"Heavy ice ahead, sir," shouted Mr Mansell, who was at the masthead with a telescope.

"Where away?"

"On the weather bow, sir, the pack seems open enough to push through, but the large bergs are numerous."

The *Hope* was now indeed getting into the heart of those icy regions where ships are in constant danger from the floating masses that come down with the ocean-currents from the far north. In sailing along she was often obliged to run with great violence against lumps so large that they caused her whole frame to tremble, stout though it was. "Shall we smash the lump, or will it stave in our bows?" was a question that frequently ran in the captain's mind. Sometimes ice closed round her and squeezed the sides so that her beams cracked. At other times, when a large field was holding her fast, the smaller pieces would grind and rasp against her as they went past, until the crew fancied the whole of the outer sheathing of planks had been scraped off. Often she had to press close to ice-bergs of great size, and more than once a lump as large as a good-sized house fell off the ice-fields and plunged into the sea close to her side, causing her to rock violently on the waves that were raised by it.

Indeed the bergs are dangerous neighbours, not only from this cause, but also on account of their turning upside down at times, and even falling to pieces, so that Captain Harvey always kept well out of their way when he could; but this was not always possible. The little brig had a narrow escape one day from the falling of a berg.

R. M. Ballantyne

It was a short time after that day on which they had the game of football. They passed in safety through the floes and bergs that had been seen that evening, and got into open water beyond, where they made made good progress before falling in with ice; but at last they came to a part of Baffin's Bay where a great deal of ice is always found. Here the pack surrounded them, and compelled them to pass close to a berg which was the largest they had fallen in with up to that time. It was jagged in form, and high rather than broad. Great peaks rose up from it like the mountain tops of some wild highland region. It was several hundred yards off the weather-beam when the brig passed, but it towered so high over the masts that it seemed to be much nearer than it was. There was no apparent motion in this berg, and the waves beat and rolled upon its base just as they do on the shore of an island. In fact it was as like an island as possible, or, rather, like a mountain planted in the sea, only it was white instead of green. There were cracks and rents and caverns in it, just as there are on a rugged mountain side, all of which were of a beautiful blue colour. There were also slopes and crags and precipices, down which the water of the melted ice constantly flowed in wild torrents. Many of these were equal to small rivulets, and some of the waterfalls were beautiful. The berg could not have measured less than a mile round the base, and it was probably two hundred feet high. It is well known that floating ice sinks deep, and that there is about eight or ten times as much of it below as there is above water. The reader may therefore form some idea of what an enormous mass of ice this berg was.

The crew of the *Hope* observed, in passing, that lumps were continually falling from the cliffs into the sea. The berg was evidently in a very rotten and dangerous state, and the captain ran the brig as close to the pack on the other side as possible, in order to keep out of its way. Just as this was done, some great rents occurred, and suddenly a mass of ice larger than the brig fell from the top of a cliff into the sea. No danger flowed from this, but the mass thus thrown off was so large as to destroy the balance of the berg, and, to the horror of the sailors, the huge mountain began to roll over. Fortunately it fell in a direction away from the brig. Had it rolled toward her, no human power could have saved our voyagers. The mighty mass went over with a wild hollow roar, and new peaks and cliffs rose out of the sea, as the old ones disappeared, with great cataracts of uplifted brine pouring furiously down their sides.

Apart from its danger, this was an awful sight. Those who witnessed it could only gaze in solemn silence. Even the most careless among them must have been forced to recognise the might and majesty of God in the event, as well as His mercy in having led them to the *right* side of the berg at such a dangerous moment.

But the scene had not yet closed. For some time the ice mountain rocked grandly to and fro, raising a considerable swell on the sea, which, all round, was covered with the foam caused by this tremendous commotion. In a few minutes several rents took place, sounding like the reports of great guns. Rotten as it was, the berg could not stand the shock of its change of position, for it had turned fairly upside down. Crack after crack took place, with deafening reports. Lumps of all sizes fell from its sides. Then there was a roar, long continued like thunder; a moment after, the whole berg sank down in ruins, and, with a mighty crash, fell flat upon the sea!

The *Hope* was beyond the reach of danger, but she rose and sank on the swell, caused by the ruin of this berg, for

R. M. Ballantyne

some time after.

It was on the afternoon of the same day that the brig received her first really severe "nip" from the ice.

She had got deep into the pack, and was surrounded on all sides by large bergs, some of these being high, like the one that has just been described, others low and flat but of great extent. One, not far off, was two miles long, and its glittering walls rose about fifteen feet above the sea. The sky was brighter than usual at the time. This was owing to one of those strange appearances which one sees more of in the Arctic regions than in any other part of the world. The sun shone with unclouded splendour, and around it there were three mock suns almost as bright as the sun itself, one on each side and one directly above it. Learned men call these bright spots *parhelia*. Sailors call them sun-dogs. They were connected together with a ring of light which entirely encircled the sun, but the lower edge of it was partly lost on the horizon.

Although this was the first time that these mock suns had been seen by Gregory and some others of the crew of the *Hope*, little attention was paid to them at the time, because of the dangerous position into which the brig had been forced. The pack had again closed all around her, obliging her to take shelter in the lee of a small berg, which, from its shape, did not seem likely to be a dangerous protector.

There was a small bay in the berg. Into this the brig was warped, and for some time she lay safely here. It was just large enough to hold her, and a long tongue of ice, projecting from the foot of it, kept off the pressure of the sea-ice. Nevertheless a look of anxiety rested on the captain's face after the ice-anchors had been made fast.

"You don't seem to like our position, captain," said young Gregory, who had been watching the doings of the men and now and then lent them a hand.

"I don't, Tom. The pack is closing tight up, and this berg may prove an enemy instead of a friend, if it forces into our harbour here. Let us hear what our mate thinks of it. What say you, Mr Mansell, shall we hold on here, or warp out and take our chance in the pack?"

"Better hold on, sir," answered the mate gravely. "The pack is beginning to grind; we should get a tight embrace, I fear, if we went out. Here we may do well enough; but everything depends on that tongue."

He looked as he spoke toward the point of ice which extended in front of the brig's stern, and guarded the harbour from the outer ice in that direction. The tongue was not a large one, and it was doubtful whether it could stand the pressure that was increasing every minute.

The pack was indeed beginning to "grind," as the mate had said, for, while they were looking at it, the edges of two floes came together with a crash about fifty yards from the berg. They ground together for a moment with a harsh growling sound, and then the two edges were suddenly forced up to a height of about fifteen or twenty feet. Next moment they fell on the closed-up ice, and lay there in a mound, or *hummock*, of broken masses.

"That's how a 'ummuck is formed, Dr Gregory," said Mr Dicey, looking uncommonly wise. "You'll see more things here in five minutes, by means of your own eyes, than ye could learn from books in a year. There's nothin' like seein'. Seein' is believin', you know. I wouldn't give an ounce of experience for a ton of hearsay."

R. M. Ballantyne

"Come, Mr Dicey, don't run down book-learning," said Gregory. "If a man only knew about things that he had seen, he would know very little."

Before the second mate could reply the captain shouted to the men to "Bear a hand with the ice-poles." The whole crew answered to the call, and each man, seizing a long pole, stood ready for action.

The tongue to which I have referred more than once had broken off, and the ice was rushing in. The bay was full in a minute, and although the men used their ice-poles actively, and worked with a will, they could not shove the pieces past them. The *Hope* was driven bow on to the berg. Then there was a strain, a terrible creaking and groaning of the timbers, as if the good little vessel were complaining of the pressure. All at once there was a loud crack, the bow of the brig lifted a little, and she was forced violently up the sloping side of the berg. Twice this happened, and then she remained stationary—high and dry out of the water!

# CHAPTER FIVE

## A GALE—NARROW ESCAPES—
## SIGNS OF WINTER—SET FAST

During the rest of that day and the whole of that night did the brig remain fixed on the berg. Early next morning the ice began to move. It eased off, and the vessel slid gently down the slope on which she had been forced, and was re-launched safely into the water.

The satisfaction of the crew, on being thus delivered from a position of much danger, was very great; but they had no sooner escaped from one peril than they were overtaken by another. A sharp breeze sprang up from the eastward, and drove them out into the pack, which began to heave about in a terrible manner under the influence of the wind. Soon this increased to a gale, and the ice was driven along at great speed by a strong northerly current.

While this was going on, land was discovered bearing to the northeast. Here was new danger, for although it was not a lee-shore, still there was some risk of the vessel being caught among grounded ice-bergs—of which a few were seen.

The gale increased to such a degree before night that

R. M. Ballantyne

Captain Harvey began to think of taking shelter under the lee of one of these bergs. He therefore stood toward one, but before reaching it the vessel received one or two severe shocks from passing floes. A large berg lay within half a mile of them. They reached it in safety, and getting under its lee, lowered a boat and fixed their ice-anchors. Just after they were fixed, a mass of ice, the size of a ship's long-boat and many tons in weight, came suddenly up out of the sea with great violence, the top of it rising above the bulwarks. One corner of it struck the hull just behind the mainmast, and nearly stove in the bottom of the brig.

This lump was what Arctic voyagers term a "calf." When masses of ice break off from the bergs far below the surface of the water, they rise with extreme violence, and ships run great risk of being destroyed by these calves when they anchor too near to the bergs. Had this calf struck the *Hope* a fair blow she must certainly have gone down with all on board.

They were not yet freed from their troubles, however. In half an hour the wind shifted a few points, but the stream of the loose ice did not change. The brig was, therefore, blown right in among the rushing masses. The three cables that held her were snapped as if they had been pieces of packthread, and she was whirled out into the pack, where she drove helplessly, exposed to the fury of the howling storm and the dangers of the grinding ice. Captain Harvey now felt that he could do nothing to save his vessel. He believed that if God did not mercifully put forth His hand to deliver them by a miracle, he and his companions would certainly perish. In this the captain was wrong. Nothing is impossible to the Almighty. He can always accomplish his purposes without the aid of a miracle.

There did, indeed, seem no way of escape; for the driving masses of ice were grinding each other to powder in nearly every direction, and the brig only escaped instant destruction by being wedged between two pieces that held together from some unknown cause. Presently they were carried down toward a large berg that seemed to be aground, for the loose ice was passing it swiftly. This was not the case, however. An undercurrent, far down in the depths of the sea, was acting on this berg, and preventing it from travelling with the ice that floated with the stream at the surface. In its passing, the mass of ice that held them struck one of the projecting tongues beneath the surface, and was split in two. The brig was at once set free. As they passed they might almost have leaped upon the berg. Captain Harvey saw and seized his opportunity.

"Stand by to heave an anchor," he shouted.

Sam Baker, being the strongest man in the ship, sprang to one of the small ice-anchors that lay on the deck with a line attached to it, and, lifting it with both hands, stood ready.

The brig passed close to the end of the berg, where the lee-side formed a long tail of sheltered water. She was almost thrust into this by the piece of ice from which she had just escaped. She grazed the edge of the berg as she drove past.

"Heave!" shouted the captain.

Sam Baker swung the anchor round his head as if it had been a feather, and hurled it far upon the ice. For a few yards it rattled over the slippery surface; then it caught a lump, but the first strain broke it off. Just after that it fell into a crack and held on. The brig was checked, and swung round into the smooth water; but they had to ease off the line lest it should snap. At last she was brought up, and lay safely under the shelter of that berg until the storm was over.

Some weeks flew by after this without anything occurring worthy of particular notice. During this time the *Hope* made good progress into the Polar regions, without again suffering severely either from ice or storm, although much retarded by the thick fogs that prevail in the Arctic regions. She was indeed almost always surrounded by ice, but it was sufficiently open to allow of a free passage through it. Many whales and seals had been seen, also one or two bears, but not in circumstances in which they could be attacked without occasioning much delay.

The brief summer had now passed away, and the days began to shorten as winter approached. Still Captain Harvey hoped to get farther north before being obliged to search for winter quarters. One morning early in September, however, he found to his sorrow that pancake-ice was forming on the sea. When the sea begins to freeze it does so in small needle-like spikes, which cross and recross each other until they form thin ice, which the motion of the waves breaks up into flat cakes about a foot or so across. These, by constantly rubbing against each other, get worn into a rounded shape. Sailors call this "pancake-ice." It is the first sign of coming winter. The cakes soon become joined together as the frost increases.

The place where this occurred was near to those wild cliffs that rise out of the sea in the channels or straits that lie at the head of Baffin's Bay. The vessel was now beyond the farthest point of land that had been discovered at the time of which I am writing, and already one or two of the headlands had been named by Captain Harvey and marked on his chart.

"I don't like to see pancake-ice so early in the season," remarked the captain to Mr Mansell.

"No more do I, sir," answered the mate. "This would be a bad place to winter in, I fear."

"Land ahead!" was shouted at that moment by the look-out at the masthead.

"Keep her away two points," said the captain to the man at the helm. "How does it lie?"

"Right ahead, sir."

"Any ice near it?"

"No; all clear."

The brig was kept a little more out to sea. Soon she came to more open water, and in the course of four hours was close to the land, which proved to be a low, barren island, not more than a mile across.

Here the wind died away altogether, and a sharp frost set in. The pancakes became joined together, and on the following morning, when our friend Gregory came on deck, he found that the whole ocean was covered with ice! It did not, indeed, look very like ice, because, being so thin, it did not prevent the usual swell from rolling over the sea. A light breeze was blowing, and the brig cut her way through it for some time; but the breeze soon died away, leaving her becalmed within a quarter of a mile of the island.

R. M. Ballantyne

For some time the voyagers hoped that a thaw would take place, or that wind would break up the ice. But they were disappointed. This was the first touch of the cold hand of winter, and the last day of the *Hope's* advance northward.

Seeing this, Captain Harvey set energetically to work to cut his way into winter quarters, for it would not do to remain all winter in the exposed position in which his vessel then lay. On his right was the island, already referred to, about a quarter of a mile off. Beyond this, about five miles distant, were the high steep cliffs of the western coast of Greenland. Everywhere else lay the open sea, covered here and there with floes and bergs, and coated with new ice.

This ice became so thick in the course of another night that the men could walk on it without danger. By means of saws and chisels made for the purpose, they cut a passage toward the island, and finally moored the brig in a small bay which was sheltered on all sides except the east. This, being the land side, required no protection. They named the place ' Refuge Harbour."

Everyone was now full of activity. The voyagers had reached the spot where they knew they were destined to spend the winter and much had to be done before they could consider themselves in a fit state to face that terrible season.

Winter in the Polar regions extends over eight months of the year—from September to May. But so much of ice and snow remains there all the summer that winter can scarcely be said to quit those regions at all.

It is difficult to imagine what the Arctic winter is. We cannot properly understand the tremendous difficulties and sufferings that men who go to the Polar seas have to fight against. Let the reader think of the following facts, and see if he does not draw his chair closer to the fire and feel thankful that he has not been born an Eskimo, and is not an Arctic seaman!

Winter within the Arctic circle, as I have said, is fully eight months long. During that time the land is covered with snow many feet deep, and the sea with ice of all degrees of thickness—from vast fields of ten or fifteen feet thick to bergs the size of islands and mountains— all frozen into one solid mass.

There is no sunlight there, night or day, for three out of these eight winter months, and there is not much during the remaining five. In summer there is perpetual sunlight, all night as well as all day, for about two months—for many weeks the sun never descends below the horizon. It is seen every day and every night sweeping a complete circle in the bright blue sky. Having been so free of his light in summer, the sun seems to think he has a right to absent himself in winter, for the three months of darkness that I have spoken of are not months of *partial* but of *total* darkness—as far, at least, as the sun is concerned. The moon and stars and the "Northern Lights" do, indeed, give their light when the fogs and clouds will allow them; but no one will say that these make up for the absence of the sun.

Then the frost is so intense that everything freezes solid except pure spirits of wine. Unless you have studied the thermometer you cannot understand the intensity of this frost; but for the sake of those who do know something about extreme cold, I give here a few facts that were noted down during the winter that my story tells of.

R. M. Ballantyne

On the 10th of September these ice-bound voyagers had eighteen degrees of frost, and the darkness had advanced on them so rapidly that it was dark about ten at night. By the 1st of October the ice round the brig was a foot and a half thick. Up to this time they had shot white hares on the island, and the hunting parties that crossed the ice to the mainland shot deer and musk oxen, and caught white foxes in traps. Gulls and other birds, too, had continued to fly around them; but most of these went away to seek warmer regions farther south. Walrus and seals did not leave so soon. They remained as long as there was any open water out at sea. The last birds that left them, (and the first that returned in spring) were the "snow-birds"— little creatures about the size of a sparrow, almost white, with a few brown feathers here and there. The last of these fled from the darkening winter on the 7th of November, and did not return until the 1st of the following May. When they left it was dark almost all day. The thermometer could scarcely be read at noon, and the stars were visible during the day. From this time forward thick darkness set in, and the cold became intense. The thermometer fell *below* zero, and after that they never saw it *above* that point for months together—20 degrees, 30 degrees, and 40 degrees below were common temperatures. The ice around them was ten feet thick. On the 1st of December noon was so dark that they could not see fifty yards ahead, and on the 15th the fingers could not be counted a foot from the eyes. The thermometer stood at 40 degrees below zero.

The darkness could not now become greater, but the cold still continued to grow more intense. It almost doubled in severity. In January it fell to 67 degrees below zero! So great was this cold that the men felt impelled to breathe gradually. The breath issued from their mouths in white clouds of steam and instantly settled on their beards and whiskers in hoar-frost. In the cabin of the *Hope* they had the utmost difficulty in keeping themselves moderately warm at this time.

Things had now reached their worst, and by slow degrees matters began to mend. On the 22nd of January the first faint sign of returning day appeared—just a blue glimmer on the horizon. By the middle of February the light tipped the tops of the mountains on shore, and the highest peaks of the ice-bergs on the sea, and on the 1st of March it bathed the deck of the *Hope*. Then the long-imprisoned crew began to feel that spring was really coming. But there was little heat in the sun's rays at first, and it was not till the month of May that the ice out at sea broke up and summer could be said to have begun.

During all this long winter—during all these wonderful changes, our Arctic voyagers had a hard fight in order to keep themselves alive. Their life was a constant struggle. They had to fight the bears and the walrus; to resist the cold and the darkness; to guard against treachery from the natives; and to suffer pains, sickness, and trials, such as seldom fall to the lot of men in ordinary climates.

How they did and suffered all this I shall try to show in the following pages. In attempting this I shall make occasional extracts from the journal of our friend Tom Gregory, for Tom kept his journal regularly, and was careful to note down only what he heard and saw.

# CHAPTER SIX

## PREPARATIONS FOR WINTERING—
## REMARKABLE ADVENTURES WITH A BEAR

The first care of Captain Harvey, after getting his brig securely laid up in her icy cradle for the winter was to remove some of the stores to the island, where he had them carefully secured in a little hut which the crew built of loose stones. This relieved the strain on the vessel, and permitted the free circulation of air. The fitting up of the interior of the brig was then begun.

The wooden partition between the cabin and the hold was taken down, and the whole space thrown into one apartment. The stove was put up in the centre of it, and moss was piled round the walls inside about a foot thick. Moss was also spread on the deck, and above it the snow was allowed to gather, for snow, although so cold itself, keeps things that it covers warm, by not permitting the heat to escape. The brig was banked up all round with snow, and a regular snowy staircase was built from the ice to her bulwarks.

They changed their time, now, from what is called sea-time to that which we follow on land. That is to say, they reckoned the day to commence just after twelve, midnight, instead of dividing it into watches, as they were wont to do at sea. Journals were begun, and careful notes made of everything that occurred, or that might in any way further the object for which they had gone there. Every man in the ship had his appointed duty and his post. If the native Eskimos should arrive in a warlike temper, each man had his cutlass and pistols in readiness. If a bear should pay them a visit, each could lay hands on his musket in an instant; and if a fire should break out on board, every man had his bucket ready and his particular post fixed. Some were to run to the water-hole, which it was the duty of one man to keep open. Others were to station themselves from the hole to the ship to pass the buckets, while the rest were to remain on board to convey them to the point of danger. Captain Harvey fixed all the arrangements, and superintended the carrying out of his orders in a general way, making his two officers and the young doctor responsible for the overseeing of details. Each of these foremen furnished him with a report every night of what had been done during the day, and the result was noted down by himself in a journal. Thus everything went smoothly and pleasantly along during the first weeks of their sojourn in their frozen home.

In regard to fresh provisions they were fortunate at first, for they obtained sufficient supplies of deer and other game. This was in the early part of winter, while there was still plenty of daylight. In Tom Gregory's journal I find it thus written:

"*September 10th.*—The days are beginning to shorten now, and we are all busily occupied in preparing for the long, dark winter that is before us. Sam Baker, who is the best shot among us, brought in a deer to-day. This is fortunate, for we stand in need of fresh meat. Our greatest enemy this winter, I fear, will be scurvy. Unless we obtain a large supply of fresh provisions we cannot hope to escape it. Crofts brought in two Arctic hares. They are beautiful creatures—pure white—and each weighs about seven pounds. These, with the four deer shot by myself last week and the ten hares got by Baker, will keep us going for some time.

"*September 12th.*—I had an adventure with a polar bear last night, which has amused the men very much, and given them food for jocularity for a few days. Some days back Davy Butts set a trap on the island, in which he has caught a few foxes. Last night his long legs were so tired that he did not care to visit his trap, so I offered to go instead of him. It was while I was out on this errand that I happened to meet with bruin. Our meeting was sudden and unexpected on both sides, I believe. It was midnight when I set off to the trap, which was not more than half a mile from the ship, and it was quite dark when I reached it.

"Davy is an ingenious fellow. His trap is made of four blocks of hard snow, with a sort of wooden trigger that goes off the moment the bait is touched, and allows a heavy log to fall down on the poor fox's back. There was no fox there, however, when I reached it. I went down on my knees and was examining the bait, when I heard a low growl. I leaped up, and felt for the knife which I usually carried in my belt. It was not there! In the haste of my departure from the ship I had forgotten to buckle it on. I had no gun, of course. It was too dark to shoot, and I had not counted on meeting with any dangerous enemy. I could only crouch down behind a lump of ice and hope that the bear would go away, but another growl, much louder than the first, and close at hand, showed that I had been seen. It was so dark that I could hardly see fifty yards ahead. There was a great chasm or hole just in front of me. This was the place where the main body of the sea-ice had been separated from the shore-ice that was aground. Here every rise and fall of the tide had broken it afresh, so that the rent was twenty yards wide, and full of large blocks that had been tossed about in confusion. Across this I gazed into the gloom, and thought I saw an object that looked like a large block of rounded ice. Before I could make up my mind how to act, the block of ice rose up with a furious roar and charged me. The chasm checked him for a moment. But for this I should have been caught immediately. While he was scrambling over it I took to my heels, and ran along the edge of the ice at the top of my speed.

"There was a narrow part of the chasm which I had looked at in daylight, and wondered whether I might venture to leap across it. I had made up my mind that it was too wide and dangerous to be attempted. But it is wonderful how quickly a man changes his mind on such a point when a polar bear is roaring at his heels. I came to the gap in the ice. It was ten feet deep and thirteen or fourteen feet across. The jagged lumps of ice at the bottom lay there in horrible confusion. There was barely light enough to see where the hole was when I came within ten yards of it, but I did not hesitate. A rush! a bound! and I went over like a cat. Not so the bear. He had not measured the place with his eye in daylight, as I had done. He made a gallant leap, it is true, but fell short, as I knew from the bursting sound and the growl of rage with which he came against the edge of the ice, and fell back among the broken blocks. I did not wait to see how he got out, you may be sure, but ran as I never ran before in all my life! I reached the brig quite out of breath. The bear had not followed me up, for I did not see him that night again. Long Davy laughed at me a good deal, and said he was sure I had been frightened at a shadow. It gave a

R. M. Ballantyne

wonderfully loud roar for a shadow! I hope that Davy himself may get a chase before the winter is over, just to convince him of his error in not believing me!"

The kind wish thus expressed in the young doctor's journal was gratified sooner than might have been expected.

Only two days after the incident above described, poor Davy Butts met with the same bear, face to face, and had a run for his life, that turned the laugh from Tom Gregory to himself.

It was on the afternoon of a clear, cold day, just about sunset. The men had finished dinner and were smoking their pipes on deck, stamping their feet and slapping their hands and arms, to keep them warm.

"Hallo, Davy! where are you bound for?" inquired the captain, on observing that Butts was wrapping himself carefully in his fur-coat, tightening his belt, and putting on his mittens as if bent on a long journey.

"I'm only goin' to take a look at my fox-trap, sir, if you'll allow me."

"Certainly, my lad. If you get a fox it's well worth the trouble. And hark'ee, Davy, take your axe and make one or two more of these snow-traps of yours. It will be a well-spent hour."

"Why, Butts," exclaimed Gregory, "what do you mean to do with that big horse-pistol? Surely you are not afraid of bears after laughing so much at the one that chased me?"

"Oh, no, not *afraid*, you know," replied Davy. "But

there's no harm in being armed."

"Mind you shoot him straight in the eye, or send a bullet up his nose. Them's the vulnerable parts of him," cried Joe Davis, with a laugh, as Butts went down the snow-steps and got upon the ice.

"I say," cried Pepper, as he was moving away.

"Well?"

"Bring his tongue aboard with you, and I'll cook it for supper."

"Ah, and a bit of fat to fry it in," added the steward. "There's nothin' like tongue fried in bear's grease."

"No, no, Dawkins," said Mr Dicey. "Hallo! Davy; bring the 'ams. Bear's 'ams are considered fustrate heatin'."

"No, *don't* bring the hams," shouted Jim Croft, "fetch the tongue; that's the thing for supper of a cold night—fetch the tongue, lad."

"Hold your own tongue," shouted Davy, in reply, as he went off amid the laughter of his comrades.

The sun sank soon after, and before the ingenious seaman had finished two new traps the short twilight had gradually deepened into night. Still there was plenty of light, for the sky was clear, and studded with a host of stars. In addition to this the Aurora Borealis was sending its beautiful flashes of pale-green light all across the western sky.

The Aurora—which also goes by the names of "Northern

R. M. Ballantyne

Lights," and "Streamers," and "Merry-dancers," is seen in great splendour in these northern skies. When the seaman had finished his traps, and looked up for a minute or two at the sky, before starting on his return to the ship, he beheld the Aurora extending over the heavens in the form of an irregular arch. It was extremely bright, but the brightness was not the same in all parts. It moved and waved gently about like a band of thin green fire. Every now and then long tongues or streamers darted up from it, and these were brighter than the rest. They were yellowish white, and sometimes became pale pink in colour. The light from this beautiful object was equal to that of the moon in her quarter, and the stars that were behind it shone dimly through, as if they were covered with a thin gauze veil.

While Davy was gazing in wonder at the splendid lights above him, a deep growl fell upon his ear. If the man had been a Jack-in-the-box he could not have leaped more quickly round. His pistol was out and cocked in a moment!

The growl was followed by a roar, which drove all the blood back into Davy's heart, and seemed to freeze it there—solid.

The man was no coward, as was quite clear, for at first he boldly stood his ground. But he would have been more than mortal if he had not felt some strange qualms about his heart when he saw a large white bear rushing furiously toward him. The animal came this time from the interior of the small island. The seaman knew well the place over which young Gregory had jumped when he had been chased. After wavering for a moment or two he turned and fled. Another tremendous roar helped him over the ice like a deer, and he took the chasm with a bound like an India-rubber ball.

It must certainly have been the same animal that chased Gregory, for, instead of trying to leap the chasm, it went to another part of the rent and scrambled across. This gave Butts time to increase the distance between them, but a man is no match for a polar bear in a race. The monster was soon close up with him, and the ship still far off. The man knew his danger; he turned, took a quick aim, and fired. He missed, of course; flung the pistol in desperation in the bear's face, and ran on. The pistol happened to stick in the snow, with the butt in the air, and when the bear came up to it he stopped to smell it!

It it well known, nowadays, that polar bears are full of curiosity, and will stop for a few minutes to examine anything that comes in their way, even when they are in full chase of a man. Davy Butts knew nothing of this at the time; but he was a quick-witted fellow. He observed this stopping of the bear, and determined to give him something more to stop at.

When bruin was close at his heels he threw down his cap. The bear at once pulled up, smelt it all round, tossed it into the air with his snout, pawed it once or twice, then tore it to pieces with one wrench, and continued the chase. Very little time was lost in this operation. He was soon up with the man again; then a mitten was thrown down for his inspection. After that the other mitten went, the cravat followed, and the axe went next. All that I have just related happened in a very few minutes. Davy was still a good quarter of a mile from the brig; everything that he could tear off his person in haste and throw down was gone, and the bear was once more coming up behind. As a last hope he pulled off his heavy fur-coat and dropped it. This seemed to be a subject of great interest to the bear,

R. M. Ballantyne

for it was longer in inspecting it than the other things. And now poor Butts went tearing along like a maniac, in his flannel shirt and trousers. He was a miserable and curious object, for his body, besides being very long, was uncommonly lanky, and his legs and arms seemed to go like the wings of a windmill. Never, since the day of his birth, had Davy Butts run at such a pace, in such light clothing, and in such severe frost!

A long line of low hummocks hid him from the brig. The moment he passed these he came in sight of her and began to yell.

"Wot on airth is yon?" exclaimed Joe Davis, who chanced to be looking over the gangway when this remarkable object appeared.

"The wild man o' the North himself, or my name aint Jim," said Crofts, turning pale.

"Why, it's Davy Butts, I do believe," cried Sam Baker, who came on deck at that moment.

Just then the bear came tearing round the end of the hummocks in full chase.

"Hurrah! hallo! ho!" roared the men, who had crowded on deck at the first note of alarm.

Sam Baker seized a heavy ash handspike about five feet long, and was on his way to meet his comrade before the others had gained the ice. They were not slow, however. Some with muskets, some with pistols and cutlasses, and some with nothing but their fists—all followed Sam, who was now far ahead.

Baker passed Davy without a remark, and ran straight at the bear, which stopped on seeing such a big, powerful man running so furiously at him, and flourishing a bludgeon that would almost have suited the hand of a giant. But polar bears are not timid. He rose on his hind legs at once, and paid no attention whatever to the tremendous crack that Sam dealt him over the skull. The blow broke the handspike in two, and the fool-hardy seaman would soon have paid for his rashness with his life had not friendly and steady hands been near. Nothing daunted, he was about to repeat the blow with the piece of the handspike that was still in his grasp, and the bear was about to seize him with its claws, each of which were full two inches long, when the first mate and Gregory came running toward him, side by side, the first armed with a rifle, the doctor with pistols.

"Too late," gasped Gregory.

"We must fire," said Mansell, "and risk hitting Sam. Here, doctor, you are a good shot; take the rifle."

The young man obeyed, dropped on one knee, and took aim, but did not fire. Sam was between him and the bear. A sudden movement changed their positions. The side of the monster came into view, and in another instant it was stretched on the ice with a bullet in his brain.

R. M. Ballantyne

# CHAPTER SEVEN

## A GREAT BATTLE WITH THE WALRUS

It need scarcely be said that there was a jovial feast that night at supper. The bear's tongue was cooked after all, but the impudent tongues of the party were not silenced, for they almost worried the life out of poor Davy for having run away from a bear.

Soon after this event the preparations for spending the winter were completed; at least as far as the fitting up of the vessel was concerned.

"This morning," writes Gregory, in his journal, "we finished housing over our Arctic home. The *Hope* is very snug, lined with moss. and almost covered with snow. A sail has been spread over the quarter-deck like an awning; it is also covered with moss and snow. This, we hope, will give much additional warmth to our house below. We all live together now, men and officers. It will require our united strength to fight successfully against that terrible enemy, John Frost. John is king of the Arctic regions, undoubtedly!

"Dawkins got a cold-bath yesterday that amused the men much and did him no harm. For some time past we have been carrying moss from the island in large bundles. Dawkins got leave to help, as he said he was sick-tired of always working among stores. He was passing close to the fire-hole with a great bundle of moss on his back, when his foot slipped, and down he went. This hole is kept constantly open. It is Baker's duty night and morning to break the ice and have it ready in case of fire. The ice on the surface was therefore thin; in a moment nothing was to be seen of poor Dawkins but his bundle! Fortunately he held tight on to it, and we hauled him out, soaked to the skin. The thermometer stood at 35 degrees below zero, the coldest day we have had up to this time; and in two minutes the unfortunate man's clothes were frozen so stiff that he could scarcely walk! We had to break the ice on his legs and arms at the joints, and even then he had to be half hoisted on board and carried below. We all dress in seal-skin and fox-skin garments now. Dawkins had on a rough coat, made of white and grey foxes; trousers of the same; boots of seal-skin, and mittens ditto. When all this was soaked and frozen he was truly a humbling sight!

"The undressing of him was a labour of difficulty as well as of love. However, when he was rubbed dry, and re-clothed, he was none the worse. Indeed, I am inclined to think he was much the better of his ducking.

"To-morrow we are to make some curious experiments with boats, sledges, and kites. The captain is anxious to take our largest boat over the ice as far to the south as possible, and leave her there with a quantity of provisions, so that we may have her to fall back upon if any misfortune should befall the brig, which I earnestly pray that God may forbid.

"Davy Butts, who is an ingenious fellow in his way, says

that we can sail a boat on the ice almost as well as on the water, and that we may drag sledges by means of kites, if we choose. The captain means to attempt a journey to the north with sledges in spring, so, if the kites answer, Butts will have done us good service. But I have my doubts.

"The nights are closing in fast; very soon we shall be without the sun altogether. But the moon is cheering us. Last night, (28th October) she swept in a complete circle round the sky *all day* as well as all night. She only touched the horizon, and then, instead of setting, she rose again, as if the frozen sea had frightened her.

"*October 30th.*—Baker came in to-day and reported open water about six miles off, and walrus sporting in it. I shall set out to-morrow on a hunt."

The hunt which the young doctor here wrote of came off the following day, but it was a very different one from what any of the men had expected.

Early in the morning, Baker, Davy Butts, and Gregory set off on foot, armed with a rifle and two muskets, besides a couple of harpoons, a whale-lance, and a long line. They also took a small sledge, which was intended to be used in hauling home the meat if they should be successful. Three hours' hard walking brought the party to the edge of the solid ice, after which they travelled on the floes that were being constantly broken by the tides, and were only joined together by ice of a night or two old. This was little more than an inch thick, so they had to advance with caution.

Presently the loud mooing of a bull walrus was heard. Its roar was something between the lowing of a bull and the bark of a large dog, but much louder, for the walrus resembles an elephant in size more than any other animal.

Soon after they came in sight of their game. Five walrus were snorting and barking in a hole which they had broken in the ice. The way in which this huge monster opens a hole when he wants to get out of the sea is to come up from below with considerable violence and send his head crashing through the ice.

The three men now became very wary. They crept on their hands and knees behind the ice-hummocks until within about a hundred yards of the brutes. Then they ascended a small hummock to take a look round and decide on their plan of operations. While lying there, flat on their faces, they took particular care to keep their heads well concealed, just raising them high enough to observe the position of the walrus. There was a sheet of flat ice between them and the hole, so that it was impossible to advance nearer without being seen. This perplexed them much, for although their bullets might hit at that distance, they would not be able to run in quick enough to use their lances, and the harpoons would be of no use at all.

While thus undecided what to do, they were unexpectedly taught a lesson in walrus-hunting that surprised them not a little.

"Hallo! there's a bear!" whispered Davy Butts, as a hairy object crawled out from behind an ice-hummock about two hundred yards from the place where they lay, and made toward the walrus in a sly, cat-like manner.

"More like a seal," observed Baker.

"A seal! why, it's a *man*!" said Gregory, in a low, excited whisper.

R. M. Ballantyne

"So it is, sure enough," said Baker; "it must be an Eskimo, though his hairy garments make him look more like a bear than a man, and as the fellow has got here before us, I suppose we must give up our claim to the brutes."

"Time enough to talk of that when the brutes are killed," said Gregory with a smile. "But lie still, lads. We will take a lesson from this fellow, who has been so earnestly staring at the walrus that he has not noticed us."

The three men lay perfectly motionless watching the native, who crept as near to the hole as he could without being seen, and then waited for a few minutes until the creatures should dive. This they were constantly doing; staying down a few moments at a time, and then coming up to breathe—for the walrus cannot live without air. He is not a fish, and although he can stay down a long time, he *must* come to the surface occasionally to breathe. In this he resembles the seal and the whale.

Presently, down they all went with a tremendous splash. Now was the moment! the Eskimo rose, ran at full speed for a few yards, then fell flat on his face, and lay quite still as if he had been shot dead. The reason of this was soon apparent. He understood the habits of the walrus, and knew that they would rise again. This they did almost the moment after, and began their snorting, bellowing, and rolling again. Once more they dived. Up got the Eskimo, ran a few yards further forward, and then fell flat down as before. In this way he got near to the hole without being seen.

The watchers observed that he carried a harpoon and a coil of thick line.

The next time the walrus dived he ran to the edge of the

hole, but now, instead of falling down, he stood quite still with the harpoon raised above his head ready to be thrown. In a few moments the monsters reappeared. Two rose close at the edge of the hole; one was a male, the other a female. They were frightfully ugly to look at. Shaking the water from his head and shoulders, the bull at once caught sight of the man who had thus suddenly appeared. At that instant the Eskimo threw up his left arm. This action, instead of frightening the brutes away, caused them to raise themselves high out of the water, in order to have a good look at the strange creature who had thus dared to disturb them in their watery home. This was just what the native wanted. It gave him a chance of driving the harpoon under the flipper of the male. The instant this was done he caught up the end of his coil and ran quickly back to the full length of the line.

The battle that now begun was perhaps one of the fiercest that was ever fought in the Arctic regions. The walrus lashed the water furiously for a second or two and dived. This checked the native, who at once stopped running, drove the sharp point of a little piece of wood into the ice, and put the loop at the end of his line over it. He pressed the loop close down to the ice with his feet, so that he could hold on when it tightened, which it did with great force. But the line was a stout one. It had been cut from the hide of a walrus, and prepared in a peculiar way for the purpose of standing a heavy strain.

The Eskimo now played the monster as an angler plays a trout. At one moment he held on, the next he eased off. The line was sometimes like a bar of iron, then it was slackened off as the animal rose and darted about. After this had happened once or twice the bull came to the surface, blowing tremendously, and began to bark and roar in great fury. The female came up at the same time.

R. M. Ballantyne

She evidently meant to stick by her partner and share his danger. The others had dived and made off at the first sign of war.

The wounded walrus was a little flurried and very angry; the female was not at all frightened, she was passionately furious! Both of them tore up the ice tables with their great ivory tusks, and glared at their enemy with an expression that there was no mistaking. The walrus is well known to be one of the fiercest animals in the world. Woe to the poor native if he had been caught by these monsters at that time.

After some minutes spent in uselessly smashing the ice and trying to get at the native, they both dived. Now came into play the Eskimo's knowledge of the animal's habits and his skill in this curious kind of warfare. Before diving they looked steadily at the man for a second, and then swam under the ice straight for the spot where he stood. The Eskimo of course could not see this, but he knew it from past experience. He therefore changed his position instantly; ran a few yards to one side, and planted his stick and loop again. This had hardly been done when the ice burst up with a loud crash; a hole of more than fifteen feet wide was made on the exact spot which the man had quitted, and the walrus appeared with a puff like that of a steam-engine, and a roar that would have done credit to a lion.

The great lumpish-looking heads and square-cut faces of the creatures looked frightful at this point in the fight. There was something like human intelligence in their malicious and brutal faces, as the water poured down their cheeks and over their bristling beards, mingled with blood and foam.

At this moment there was a shout close at hand, and two other Eskimos ran out from behind the ice-hummocks and joined their comrade. They were armed with long lances, the handles of which were made of bone, and the points of beautiful white ivory tipped with steel. It was afterwards discovered that these natives obtained small pieces of iron and steel from the Eskimos further south, who were in the habit of trading at the settlements on the coast of Greenland.

The strangers at once ran to the edge of the pool and gave the bull walrus two deep wounds with their lances. They also wounded the female. This seemed to render them more furious than ever. They dived again. The first Eskimo again shifted his position, and the others ran back a short distance. They were not a moment too soon in these changes, for the ice was again burst upward at the spot they had just quitted, and the enraged beasts once more came bellowing to the surface and vented their fury on the ice.

It may seem almost incredible to the reader, *but it is a fact*, that this battle lasted fully four hours. At the end of the third hour it seemed to the sailors who were watching it, that the result was still doubtful, for the Eskimos were evidently becoming tired, while the monsters of the Polar seas were still furious.

"I think we might help them with a butlet," whispered Baker. "It might frighten them, perhaps, but it would save them a good deal of trouble."

"Wait a little longer," replied Gregory. "I have it in my mind to astonish them. You see they have wounded the female very badly, but when the male dies, which he cannot now be long of doing, she will dive and make off, and so they'll lose her, for they don't seem to have another harpoon and line."

"Perhaps they have one behind the hummocks," suggested Davy Butts, whose teeth were chattering in his head with cold.

"If they had they would have used it long ago," said Gregory. "At any rate I mean to carry out my plan—which is this. When the bull is about dead I will fire at the female and try to hit her in a deadly part, so as to kill her at once. Then, Sam, you will run out with our harpoon and dart into her to prevent her sinking, or diving if she should not be killed. And you, Davy, will follow me and be ready with a musket "

This plan had just been settled when the bull walrus began to show signs of approaching death. Gregory therefore took a deliberate aim with the rifle and fired. The result was startling! The female walrus began to roll and lash about furiously, smashing the ice and covering the sea around with bloody foam. At first the Eskimos stood motionless—rooted to the spot, as if they had been thunderstruck. But when they saw Sam Baker dart from behind the hummock, flourishing his harpoon, followed by Gregory and Butts, their courage deserted them; they turned in terror and fled.

On getting behind the hummocks, however, they halted and peeped over the ledges of ice to see what the seamen did.

Sam Baker, being an old whaleman, darted his harpoon cleverly, and held fast the struggling animal. At the same time Davy Butts seized the end of the line which the natives had thrown down in terror, and held on to the bull.

It was almost dead, and quite unable to show any more fight. Seeing that all was right, Gregory now laid down his rifle and advanced slowly to the hummock, behind which the Eskimos had taken refuge.

He knew, from the reports of previous travellers, that holding up both arms is a sign of peace with the Eskimos. He therefore stopped when within a short distance of the hummocks and held up his arms. The signal was understood at once. The natives leaped upon the top of the hummock and held up their arms in reply. Again Gregory tossed up his, and made signs to them to draw near. This they did without hesitation, and the doctor shook them by the hand and patted their hairy shoulders. They were all of them stout, well-made fellows, about five feet seven or eight inches high, and very broad across the shoulders. They were fat, too, and oily-faced, jolly-looking men. They smiled and talked to each other for a few moments and then spoke to Gregory, but when he shook his head, as much as to say, "I don't understand you," they burst into a loud laugh. Then they suddenly became grave, and ran at full speed toward the hole where the walrus floated.

Davy Butts made the usual sign of friendship and handed them the end of their line, which they seized, and set about securing their prize without taking any farther notice of their new friends.

The manner in which these wild yet good-natured fellows hauled the enormous carcass out of the water was simple and ingenious. They made four cuts in the neck, about two inches apart from each other, and raised the skin between these cuts, thus making two bands. Through one of these bands they passed a line, and carried it to a stick made fast in the ice, where they passed it through a loop of well-greased hide. It was then carried back to the animal, made to pass under the second band, and the end was hauled in by the Eskimos. This formed a sort of double purchase, that enabled them to pull out of the hole a carcass which double their numbers could not have hauled up.

Some idea of the bull's weight may be formed when I say that the carcass was eighteen feet long and eleven feet in circumference at the thickest part. There were no fewer than sixty deep lance-wounds in various parts of its body.

When seen close at hand the walrus is a very ugly monster. It is something like a gigantic seal, having two large flippers, or fins, near its shoulders, and two others behind, that look like its tail. It uses these in swimming, but can also use them on land, so as to crawl, or rather to bounce forward in a clumsy fashion. By means of its fore-flippers it can raise itself high out of the water, and get upon the ice and rocks. It is fond of doing this, and is often found sleeping in the sunshine on the ice and on rocks. It has even been known to scramble up the side of an island to a height of a hundred feet, and there lie basking in the sun.

Nevertheless, the water is the proper element of the walrus. All its motions are clumsy and slow until it gets into the sea; there it is "at home." Its upper face has a square, bluff look, and its broad muzzle and cheeks are covered by a coarse beard of bristles, like quills. The two white tusks point downward. In this they are unlike to those of the elephant. The tusks of the bull killed on this occasion were thirty inches long. The hide of the walrus is nearly an inch thick, and is covered with close, short hair. Beneath the skin he has a thick layer of fat, and this enables him to resist the extreme cold in the midst of which he dwells.

The walrus is of great value to the Eskimos. But for it and the seal these poor members of the human family could not exist at all in those frozen regions. As it is, it costs them a severe struggle to keep the life in their bodies. But they do not complain of what seems to us a hard lot. They have been born to it. They know no happier condition of life. They wish for no better home, and the All-wise Creator has fitted them admirably, both in mind and body, to live and even to enjoy life in a region where most other men could live only in great discomfort, if they could exist at all.

The Eskimos cut the walrus' thick hide into long lines with which they hunt—as we have seen. They do not cut these lines in strips and join them in many places; but, beginning at one end of the skin, they cut round and round without break to the centre, and thus secure a line of many fathoms in length.

It is truly said that "necessity is the mother of invention." These natives have no wood. Not a single tree grows in the whole land of which I am writing. There are plenty of plants, grasses, mosses, and beautiful flowers in summer —growing, too, close beside ice-fields that remain unmelted all the year round. But there is not a tree large enough to make a harpoon of. Consequently the Eskimos are obliged to make sledges of bones; and as the bones and tusks of the walrus are not big enough for this purpose, they tie and piece them together in a remarkably neat and ingenious manner.

Sometimes, indeed, they find pieces of drift-wood in the sea. Wrecks of whale-ships, too, are occasionally found by the natives in the south of Greenland. A few pieces of the precious wood obtained in this way are exchanged from one tribe to another, and so find their way north. But the further north we go the fewer pieces of this kind of wood do we find; and in the far north, where our adventurous voyagers were now ice-bound, the Eskimos have very little wood, indeed.

Food is the chief object which the Eskimo has in view when he goes out to do battle with the walrus. Its flesh is somewhat coarse, no doubt, but it is excellent, nourishing food notwithstanding, and although a well-fed English-man might turn up his nose at it, many starving Englishmen have smacked their lips over walrus-beef in days gone by—aye, and have eaten it raw, too, with much delight!

Let not my reader doubt the truth of this. Well-known and truth-loving men have dwelt for a time in those regions, and some of these have said that they actually came to *prefer* the walrus flesh raw, because it was more streng-thening, and fitted them better for undertaking long and trying journeys in extremely cold weather. One of the most gallant men who ever went to the Polar seas, (Dr Kane, of the American navy), tells us, in his delightful book, "Arctic Explorations", that he frequently ate raw flesh and liked it, and that the Eskimos often eat it raw. In fact, they are not particular. They will eat it cooked or raw—just as happens to be most convenient for them.

When the animals, whose killing I have described, were secured, the Eskimos proceeded to skin and cut them up. The sailors, of course, assisted, and learned a lesson. While this was going on one of their number went away for a short time, and soon returned with a sledge drawn by about a dozen dogs. This they loaded with the meat and hide of the bull, intending evidently to leave the cow to their new friends, as being their property. But Gregory thought they were entitled to a share of it, so, after loading his sledge with a considerable portion of the meat, he gave them the remainder along with the hide.

This pleased them mightily, and caused them to talk much, though to little purpose. However, Gregory made good use of the language of signs. He also delighted them with the gift of a brass ring, an old knife, and a broken pencil-case, and made them understand that his abode was not far distant, by drawing the figure of a walrus in a hole in the snow, and then a thing like a bee-hive at some distance from it, pointing northward at the same time. He struck a harpoon into the outline of the walrus, to show that it was the animal that had just been killed, and then went and lay down in the picture of the bee-hive, to show that he dwelt there.

The natives understood this quite well. They immediately drew another bee-hive, pointed to the south and to the sun, and held up five fingers. From this it was understood that their village was five days distant from the spot where they then were.

He next endeavored to purchase three of their dogs, but they objected to this, and refused to accept of three knives as a price for them. They were tempted, however, by the offer of a whale harpoon and a hemp line, and at last agreed to let him have three of their best dogs. This the young doctor considered a piece of great good fortune, and being afraid that they would repent, he prepared to leave the place at once. The dogs were fastened by lines to the sledge of their new masters. A whip was made out of a strip of walrus hide, a bone served for a handle, and away they went for the brig at a rattling pace, after bidding the natives farewell, and making them understand that they hoped to meet again in the course of the winter.

R. M. Ballantyne

Thus happily ended their first meeting with the Eskimos. It may well be believed that there were both astonishment and satisfaction on board the *Hope* that night, when the hunting party returned, much sooner than had been expected, with the whip cracking, the men cheering, the dogs howling, and the sledge well laden with fresh meat.

# CHAPTER EIGHT

## THE CAUSE OF ICE-BERGS—
## FOX-CHASE—A BEAR

One day, long after the walrus-hunt just described, Joe Davis stood on the deck of the *Hope*, leaning over the side and looking out to sea—at least in the direction of the sea, for, although mid-day, it was so dark that he could not see very far in any direction. Joe was conversing with Mr Dicey on the appearance of things around him.

"Do you know, Mr Dicey," said he, "wot it is as causes them there ice-bergs?"

Mr Dicey looked very grave and wise for a few seconds without answering. Then he said, in rather a solemn tone, "Well, Davis, to tell you the real truth, I *don't* know!"

Now, as this question is one of considerable interest, I shall endeavour to answer it for the benefit of the reader.

The whole of the interior of Greenland is covered with ice and snow. This snowy covering does not resemble that soft snow which falls on our own hills. It is hard, and *never* melts entirely away. The snow there is in some places a thousand feet thick! It covers all the hill-tops and

R. M. Ballantyne

fills up all the valleys, so that the country may be said to be a buried land. Since the world began, perhaps, snow has been falling on it every winter; but the summers there have been so short that they could not melt away the snow of one winter before that of another came and covered it up and pressed it down. Thus, for ages, the snow of one year has been added to that which was left of the preceding, and the pressure has been so great that the mass has been squeezed nearly as hard as pure ice.

The ice that has been formed in this way is called *glacier*; and the glaciers of Greenland cover, as I have said, the whole country, so that it can never be cultivated or inhabited by man unless the climate change. There are glaciers of this kind in many other parts of the world. We have them in Switzerland and in Norway, but not on nearly so large a scale as in Greenland.

Now, although this glacier-ice is clear and hard, it is not quite so solid as pure ice, and when it is pushed down into the valleys by the increasing masses above it, actually *flows*. But this flowing motion cannot be seen. It is like the motion of the hour hand of a watch, which cannot be perceived however closely it may be looked at. You might go to one of the valleys of Greenland and gaze at a glacier for days together, but you would see no motion whatever. All would appear solid, frozen up, and still. But notice a block of stone lying on the surface of the glacier, and go back many months after and you will find the stone lying a little further down the valley than when you first saw it. Thus glaciers are formed and thus they slowly move. But what has all this to do with ice-bergs? We shall see.

As the great glaciers of the north, then, are continually moving down the valleys, of course their ends are pushed into the sea. These ends, or tongues, are often hundreds of feet thick. In some places they present a clear glittering wall to the sea of several hundreds of feet in height, with perhaps as much again lost to view down in the deep water. As the extremities of these tongues are shoved farther and farther out they chip off and float away. *These chips are ice-bergs*! I have already said that ice-bergs are sometimes miles in extent—like islands; that they sink seven or eight hundred feet below the surface, while their tops rise more than a hundred feet above it—like mountains. If these, then, are the "chips" of the Greenland glaciers, what must the "old blocks" be?

Many a long and animated discussion the sailors had that winter in the cabin of the *Hope* on the subject of ice and ice-bergs!

When the dark nights drew on, little or nothing could be done outside by our voyagers, and when the ice everywhere closed up, all the animals forsook them except polar bears, so that they ran short of fresh provisions. As months of dreary darkness passed away, the scurvy, that terrible disease, began to show itself among the men, their bodies became less able to withstand the cold, and it was difficult for them at last to keep up their spirits. But they fought against their troubles bravely.

Captain Harvey knew well that when a man's spirits go he is not worth much. He therefore did his utmost to cheer and enliven those around him.

One day, for instance, he went on deck to breathe a mouthful of fresh air. It was about eleven in the forenoon, and the moon was shining brightly in the clear sky. The stars, too, and the aurora borealis, helped to make up for the total absence of the sun. The cold air cut like a knife

R. M. Ballantyne

against his face when he issued from the hatchway, and the cold nose of one of the dogs immediately touched his hand, as the animal gambolled round him with delight; for the extreme severity of the weather began to tell on the poor dogs, and made them draw more lovingly to their human companions.

"Ho! hallo!" shouted the captain down the hatchway. "A fox-chase! a fox-chase! Tumble up, all hands!"

The men were sitting at the time in a very dull and silent mood. They were much cast down, for as it had been cloudy weather for some weeks past, thick darkness had covered them night and day, so that they could not tell the one from the other, except by the help of their watches, which were kept carefully going. Their journals, also, were written up daily, otherwise they must certainly have got confused in their time altogether!

In consequence of this darkness the men were confined almost entirely to the cabin for a time. Those who had scurvy, got worse; those who were well, became gloomy. Even Pepper, who was a tremendous joker, held his tongue, and Joe Davis, who was a great singer, became silent. Jim Crofts was in his bunk "down" with the scurvy, and stout Sam Baker, who was a capital teller of stories, could not pluck up spirit enough to open his mouth. "In fact," as Mr Dicey said, "they all had a most 'orrible fit o' the blues!" The captain and officers were in better health and spirits than the men, though they all fared alike at the same table, and did the same kind of work, whatever that might chance to be. The officers, however, were constantly exerting themselves to cheer the men, and I have no doubt that this very effort of theirs was the means of doing good to themselves. "He that watereth others shall be watered," says the Word of God. I take this to mean—he that does good to others shall get good to himself. So it certainly was with the officers of the *Hope*.

When the captain's shout reached the cabin Jim Crofts had just said: "I'll tell 'ee what it is, messmates, if this here state of things goes on much longer, I'll go out on the floes, walk up to the first polar bear I meet, and ask him to take his supper off me!"

There was no laugh at this, but Pepper remarked, in a quiet way, that "he needn't put himself to so much trouble, for he was such a pale-faced, disagreeable looking object that no bear would eat him unless it was starving."

"Well, then, I'll offer myself to a starvin' bear—to one that's a'most dead with hunger," retorted Jim gloomily.

"What's that the cap'en is singin' out?" said Davy Butts, who was mending a pair of canvas shoes.

The men roused themselves at once; for the hope of anything new turning up excited them.

"Hallo! ho!" roared the captain again, in a voice that might have started a dead walrus. "Tumble up, there!—a fox-chase! I'll give my second-best fur-coat to the man that catches foxey!"

In one instant the whole crew were scrambling up the ladder. Even Jim Crofts, who was really ill, rolled out of his bunk and staggered on deck, saying he would have a "go after foxey if he should die for it!"

The game of fox is simple. One man is chosen to be the fox. He runs off and the rest follow. They are bound to go wherever the fox leads. In this case it was arranged that

R. M. Ballantyne

the fox should run round the deck until he should be caught; then the man who caught him should become fox, and continue running on with all the rest following, until he, in turn, should be caught, and so on until the one who could run longest and fastest should break down all the rest. The warm fur-coat was a prize worth running for in such a cold climate, so the game began with spirit. Young Gregory offered to be fox first, and away they went with a yell. Mr Mansell was a little lame, and soon gave in. Mr Dicey fell at the second round, and was unable to recover distance. Gregory would certainly have gained the coat, for he was strong, and had been a crack racer at school; but he did not want the coat, so allowed Sam Baker to catch him. Sam held on like a deer for a few minutes, and one after another the men dropped off as they were blown. Jim Crofts, poor fellow, made a gallant burst, but his limbs refused to help his spirit. He fell, and was assisted below by the captain and replaced in his bunk, where, however, he felt the benefit of his efforts.

The race was now kept up by Sam Baker, Joe Davis, and Butts. These three were struggling on and panting loudly, while their comrades danced about, clapped their mittened hands, and shouted, "Now then, Sam!—go in and win, Joe!—Butts, forever!" and such-like encouraging cries.

To the surprise of everyone Davy Butts came off the winner, and for many a day after that enjoyed the warm coat which he said his long legs had gained for him.

This effort of the captain to cheer the men was very successful, so he resolved to follow it up with an attempt at private theatricals. Accordingly this thing was proposed and heartily agreed to. Next day everyone was busy making preparations. Tom Gregory agreed to write a short play. Sam Baker, being the healthiest man on board, was willing to act the part of an invalid old lady, and Jim Crofts consented to become a gay young doctor for that occasion.

Meanwhile the captain arranged a piece of real work, for he felt that the attempt to keep up the spirits alone would not do. They had been for a long time living on salt provisions. Nothing could restore the crew but fresh meat—yet fresh meat was not to be had. The walrus and deer were gone, and although foxes and bears were still around them, they had failed in all their attempts to shoot or trap any of these animals. A visit to the Eskimo camp, therefore, (if such a camp really existed), became necessary; so, while the theatricals were in preparation, a small sledge was rigged up, Gregory and Sam Baker were chosen to go with him; the dogs were harnessed, and, on a fine, starry forenoon, away they went to the south at full gallop, with three hearty cheers from the crew of the brig, who were left in charge of the first mate.

The journey thus undertaken was one full of risk. It was not known how far distant the natives might be, or where they were likely to be found. The weather was intensely cold. Only a small quantity of preserved meat could be taken—for the rest, they trusted in some measure to their guns. But the captain's great hope was to reach the Eskimo village in a day or two at the farthest. If he should fail to do so, the prospect of himself and his crew surviving the remainder of the long winter was, he felt, very gloomy indeed.

Success attended this expedition at the very beginning. They had only been eight hours out when they met a bear sitting on its haunches behind a hummock. "Hallo! look out!" cried Gregory, on catching sight of him. "Fire, lads," said the captain, "I'm not quite ready." Gregory fired and

R. M. Ballantyne

the bear staggered. Baker then fired and it fell!

This was a blessing which filled their hearts so full of thankfulness that they actually shook hands with each other, and then gave vent to three hearty cheers. Their next thoughts were given to their comrades in the *Hope*.

"You and Baker will camp here, Tom," said the captain, "and I will return to the brig with a sledge-load of the meat. When I've put it aboard I'll come straight back to you. We'll keep a ham for ourselves, of course. Now then, to work."

To work the three men went. A hind leg of the bear was cut off, the rest was lashed firmly on the sledge, and the dogs enjoyed a feed while this was being done. Then the captain cracked his whip. "Good-bye, lads", "Good-bye, captain," and away he and the dogs and sledge went, and were soon lost to view among the hummocks of the frozen sea.

# CHAPTER NINE

## A VISIT TO THE ESKIMOS—
## WONDERFUL DOINGS—A MYSTERY

The proceedings of this sledge party were so interesting that I give them in the words of Tom Gregory's journal:

"*Sunday.*—We have indeed cause to rejoice and to thank God for His mercies this morning. Last night we shot a bear, and the captain is away with the carcass of it to our poor scurvy-smitten friends in the *Hope*. This Sunday will be a real day of rest for me and Sam Baker, though our resting-place is a very queer one. After the captain left us, we looked about for a convenient place to encamp, and only a few yards from the spot where we killed the bear we found the ruins of an old Eskimo hut made partly of stones, partly of ice. We set to work to patch it up with snow, and made it perfectly air-tight in about two hours.

"Into this we carried our bear-skins and things, spread them on the snowy floor, put a lump of bear's fat into our tin travelling lamp, and prepared supper. We were not particular about the cookery. We cut a couple of huge slices off our bear's ham, half roasted them over the lamp, and began. It was cut, roast, and come again, for the next hour and a half. I positively never knew what hunger was until I came to this savage country! And I certainly never before had any idea of how much I could eat at one sitting!

"This hearty supper was washed down with a swig of melted snow-water. We had some coffee with us, but were too tired to infuse it. Then we blocked up the door with snow, rolled our bear-skins round us, and were sound asleep in five minutes.

"Lucky for us that we were so careful to stop up every hole with snow, for, during the night the wind rose and it became so intensely cold that Baker and I could scarcely keep each other warm enough to sleep, tired though we were. At this moment my fingers are so stiff that they will hardly hold the pencil with which I write, and the gale is blowing so furiously outside that we dare not open the door. This door, by the way, is only a hole big enough to creep through. The captain cannot travel to-day. He knows we are safe, so I will not expect him. I have brought my small Testament with me. It has hitherto been my constant travelling companion. I am thus provided with mental food. But, in truth, I shall not want much of that for the next twelve hours. Rest! rest! rest! is what we require. No one can imagine how a man can enjoy rest, after he has been for many months exposed to constant, exhausting, heart-breaking toil, with the thermometer *always* below zero, and with nothing but salt food to keep him alive.

"*Tuesday night.*—Here we are at last—among the Eskimos! and what a queer set they are, to be sure. All fat and fur! They look as broad as they are long. They wear short fox and seal-skin coats, or shirts, with hoods to then; no trousers, but long boots, that come up and meet the coats. Women, men, and babies, all dressed alike, or nearly so. The only difference is that the women's boots are longer and wider than those of the men. But I forgot— yes, there is one other difference; the women have *tails* to their coats; the men have none! Real tails—not like the broad skirts of our dress-coats, but long, narrow tails, something like the tail of a cow, with a broadish flap at the end of it. This they evidently look upon as a handsome ornament, for I observe that when they go off on a journey, each woman buttons her tail up to her waist, to keep it out of the way, and when she returns she unbuttons it, and comes into camp with her tail flowing gracefully behind her!

"We had a terrible journey of it down here. The captain returned to us on Monday morning early, and the next two days we spent struggling over the hummocks and out upon the floes. It was so cold that the wind cut into our very marrow. We have all had our faces frozen, more or less, but not badly. Baker will have an ugly spot on the end of his nose for some weeks to come. It is getting black now, and as the nose itself is bright red and much swelled, his appearance is not improved. I foolishly tried to eat a little snow yesterday morning, and the conesquence is that my lips are sore and bloody. On Monday afternoon the dogs and sledge went head over heels into a deep rut in the ice, and it cost us two hours to get them out again. Luckily no damage was done, although the captain was on the sledge at the time.

"We had almost despaired of finding the village when we came upon a sledge track that led us straight up to it. I shall never forget the beauty of the scene on our arrival. The sky was lighted up with the most beautiful aurora I have yet seen in these regions. Stars spangled the sky in millions. Great ice-bergs rose in wild confusion in the distance, and all along the shore for a few hundred yards

R. M. Ballantyne

were clusters of snow-huts. They looked exactly like bee-hives. I have seen many a strange house, but the strangest of all is certainly a house of snow! To-day I was fortunate enough to see one built. It was done very neatly. The hard snow was cut into slabs with a wooden knife. These were piled one above another in regular order, and cemented with snow—as bricks are with lime. The form of the wall was circular, and the slabs were so shaped that they sloped inwards, thus forming a dome, or large bee-hive, with a key-stone slab in the top to keep all firm. A hole was then cut in the side for a door—just large enough to admit of a man creeping through. In front of this door a porch or passage of snow was built. The only way of getting into the hut is by creeping on hands and knees along the passage. A hole was also cut in the roof, into which was inserted a piece of clear ice, to serve for a window.

"The natives received us with wild surprise, and I found my old friends, the walrus-hunters, among them. They were remarkably friendly. One stout, middle-aged fellow invited us to his hut. I am now seated in it beside the Eskimo's wife, who would be a good-looking woman if she were not so fat, dirty, and oily! But we cannot expect people living in this fashion, and in such a country, to be very clean. Although the hut is white outside, it is by no means white inside. They cook all their food over an oil-lamp, which also serves to heat the place; and it is wonderful how warm a house of snow becomes. The cold outside is so great as to prevent the walls melting inside. Besides Myouk, our host, and his wife, there are two of the man's sisters, two lads, two girls, and a baby in the hut. Also six dogs. The whole of them—men, women, children, and dogs, are as fat as they can be, for they have been successful in walrus-hunting of late. No wonder that the perspiration is running down my face! The natives feel the heat, too, for they are all half-naked—the baby entirely so; but they seem to like it!

"What a chattering, to be sure! I am trying to take notes, and Myouk's wife is staring at me with her mouth wide open. It is a wonder she can open her eyes at all, her cheeks are so fat. The captain is trying, by the language of signs, to get our host to understand that we are much in want of fresh meat. Sam Baker is making himself agreeable to the young people, and the plan he has hit upon to amuse them is to show them his watch, and let them hear it tick. Truly, I have seldom seen a happier family group than this Eskimo household, under their snowy roof!

"There is to be a grand walrus-hunt to-morrow. We shall accompany them, and see whether our endurance on a long march, and our powers with the rifle, cannot impress them with some respect for us. At present they have not much. They seem to think us a pale-faced set of helpless creatures.

"*Wednesday night.*—We have just returned from the hunt; and a tremendous hunt it was! Six walrus and two bears have been killed, and the whole village is wild with delight. Cooking is going on in every hut. But they have no patience. Nearly everyone is munching away at a lump of raw walrus flesh. All their faces are more or less greasy and bloody. Even Myouk's baby—though not able to speak—is choking itself with a long, stringy piece of blubber. The dogs, too, have got their share. An Eskimo's chief happiness seems to be in eating, and I cannot wonder at it, for the poor creatures have hard work to get food, and they are often on the verge of starvation.

"What a dirty set they are! I shall never forget the

R. M. Ballantyne

appearance of Myouk's hut when we entered it this evening after returning from the hunt. The man's wife had made the wick of her stone lamp as long as possible in order to cook a large supper. There were fifteen people crowded together in this hive of snow, and the heat had induced them to throw off the greater part of their clothing. Every hand had a greasy lump of bear or walrus meat in it; every mouth was in full occupation, and every fat face, of man, woman, and child, was beaming with delight and covered with dirt and oil!

"The captain and I looked at each other and smiled as we entered, and Sam Baker laughed outright. This set all the natives laughing, too. We did not much relish the idea of supping and sleeping in such a place—but necessity has no law. We were hungry as hawks, desperately tired, and the temperature outside is 35 degrees below zero. The first duty of the night is now over. We have supped. The natives will continue to eat the greater part of the night. They eat till they fall asleep; if they chance to awake they eat again. Half of them are asleep now, and snoring. The other half are eating slowly, for they are nearly full. The heat and smell are awful! I am perspiring at every pore. We have taken off as much of our clothes as decency will permit. Sam has on a pair of trousers—nothing more. I am in the same state! There is little room, as may be supposed. We have to lie huddled up as we best can, and a strange sight we are as the red light of the flaring lamp falls on us. At this moment Myouk's wife is cutting a fresh steak. The youngest boy is sound asleep with a lump of fat between his teeth. The captain is also sound, with his legs sprawling over the limbs of half a dozen slumbering natives. He is using the baby as a pillow. It is curious to think that these poor creatures always live in this way. Sometimes feasting, sometimes starving. Freezing out on the floes; stewing under their roofs of snow.

Usually fat; for the most part jolly; always dirty!

"It is sad, too, to think of this; for it is a low condition for human beings to live in. They seem to have no religion at all. Certainly none that is worthy of the name. I am much puzzled when I think of the difficulties in the way of introducing Christianity among these northern Eskimos. No missionary could exist in such a climate and in such circumstances. It is with the utmost difficulty that hardy seamen can hold out for a year, even with a ship-load of comforts. But this is too deep a subject to write about to-night! I can't keep my eyes open. I will, therefore, close my note-book and lie down to sleep—perhaps to be suffocated! I hope not!"

Accordingly, our young friend the doctor did lie down to sleep, and got through the night without being suffocated. Indeed, he slept so soundly that Captain Harvey could scarcely rouse him next morning.

"Hallo! Tom! Tom!" cried he loudly, at the same time shaking his nephew's arm violently.

"Aye, eh!" and a tremendous yawn from Tom. "What now, uncle? Time to rise, is it? Where am I?"

"Time to rise!" replied the captain, laughing. "I should think it is. Why, it's past eleven in the forenoon. The stars are bright and the sky clear. The aurora, too, is shining. Come, get up! The natives are all outside watching Sam while he packs our sledge. The ladies are going about the camp whisking their tails and whacking their babies in great glee, for it is not every day they enjoy such a feed as they had last night."

In half an hour they were ready. The whole village turned

R. M. Ballantyne

out to see them start. Myouk, with his wife Oomia, and the baby, and his son Meetek, accompanied them to Refuge Harbour. Oomia's baby was part of herself. She could not move without it! It was always naked, but being stuffed into the hood of its mother's fur-coat, it seemed always warm.

"I say, Tom, what's that up in the sky?" said Captain Harvey suddenly, after they had been driving for a couple of hours. "It's the strangest looking thing I ever did see."

"So it is," replied Gregory, gazing intently at the object in question, which seemed high up in the air. "It can't be a comet, because it gives no light."

"Perhaps not, but it has got a tail, that's a fact," said Baker, in a voice of surprise. "Who ever heard of a dark, four-cornered star with a tail? If I had seen it in daylight, and in Merry England, I would have said it was a kite!"

"A kite! nonsense," cried the captain; "what in the world *can* it be?"

Reader, you shall find that out in the next chapter.

# CHAPTER TEN

## THE TALE OF A KITE—A GREAT BEAR-FIGHT

When Mr Mansell was left in charge of the brig a heavy weight lay on his heart, and he could by no means take part in the preparations for the theatricals which occupied the rest of the crew. He felt that life or death depended on the success of the captain in his search for fresh meat. Already most of the men were ill with scurvy, and some of them were alarmingly low. Nothing could save them but fresh meat, and when the first mate thought of the difficulties and dangers of a journey on the floes in such weather, and the uncertainty of the Eskimos being discovered, his heart misgave him.

About an hour after the departure of Captain Harvey on the Monday morning he took Davy Butts aside.

"Davy," said he, "you've been at work on these kites a long time. Are they nearly finished?"

"Quite finished, sir," answered Butts.

"Then get them up, for there is a good breeze. I shall try them on our small sledges. It will at least stir up and amuse the men."

Ten minutes after this the crew were summoned on deck to witness an experiment. A small dog sledge lay on the hard snow beside the vessel, and near to this Davy Butts and Mr Dicey were holding on to a stout line, at the end of which an enormous kite was pulling.

This kite was square in shape, made of the thickest brown paper, and nearly six feet across. That its power was great was evident from the difficulty with which the two men held it. The end of the line was fastened to the sledge.

"Now, boys, ease off line till it is taut, and then wait for the word," said Davy Butts, jumping on to the sledge. "Now! Let go!"

Away went the sledge over the hard snow at the rate of three miles an hour, which soon increased to double that rate. Davy cheered and waved his arms. The men gave one loud "hurrah" of surprise and delight, and set off in mad pursuit. They were soon left behind. "Hold on, Davy!" "Good-bye, Butts." "Look out, mind the ridge!"

The last warning was needful. The sledge was rushing furiously toward a long ridge of ice which rose in a sharp slope to a height of three feet, and descended on the other side to an equal depth, but without any slope. Davy saw his danger, but he did not dare to put out foot or hand to check his progress. Even if he had it would have been of no use. Up the slope he went as a sea-gull skims over a wave; for one moment he was in the air—the next, he came down with a crash that nearly dislocated all his joints, and his teeth came together with a loud snap. (By good fortune his tongue was not between them!) The sledge was a strong one, and the thing was done so quickly and neatly that it did not upset. But now a large and rugged hummock lay right before him. To go against that would have been certain death, so Davy made up his mind at once, and jumped off at the smoothest part of the floe he could find. The lightened sledge sprang away like a rocket, and was brought up with a sudden jerk by the hummock.

Of course the line broke, and the kite commenced to descend. It twirled and circled violently round, and at last went crash into an ice-berg, where it was broken to pieces!

"Not so bad for a beginning," said Mansell, as poor Davy came back, looking very crest-fallen. "Now, Butts, come below. You have proved that the thing will do. Mr Dicey, get yourself ready for a trip over the ice. Let three men prepare to accompany you. I shall send you off to-morrow."

Dicey, much surprised, went off to obey these orders; and Mansell, with the assistance of Butts, fitted the second kite for the intended journey. He made a rough guess at the strength of its pull, and loaded the sledge accordingly. Two tail ropes were fastened to the last bar of the sledge for the men to hold on by and check its speed. A sort of anchor was made by which it could be stopped at any moment, and two stout poles, with iron claws at the end of them, were prepared for scraping over the snow and checking the pace.

Next day all was ready. A trial was made and the thing found to work admirably. The trial trip over, they bade their comrades farewell, and away they went due south, in the direction where the native village was supposed to be.

It was this remarkable tow-horse that had filled Captain Harvey and his companions with so much surprise. The appearance of the sledge immediately after, with a shout and a cheer from Dicey and the men, explained the mystery.

Being so near the Eskimo camp they at once returned to it, in order to allow the newly arrived party to rest, as well as to load their sledge with as much fresh meat as it could carry; for which supplies the captain took care to pay the natives with a few knives and a large quantity of hoop-iron—articles that were much more valuable to them than gold. As the wind could not be made to turn about to suit their convenience, the kite was brought down and given to Davy to carry, and a team of native dogs were harnessed to the sledge instead. On the following day the united party set out on their return to the brig, which they reached in safety.

Tom Gregory's account of the Eskimos who accompanied them to their wooden home is amusing. His journal runs thus:

"The amazement of our visitors is very great. Myouk, his wife and baby, and his son Meetek, are now our guests. When they first came in sight of the brig they uttered a wild shout—the men did so, at least—and tossed their arms and opened their eyes and mouths. They have never shut them since. They go all round the vessel, staring and gaping with amazement. We have given them a number of useful presents, and intend to send them home loaded with gifts for their friends. It is necessary to make a good impression on them. Our lives depend very much on the friendship of these poor people. We find that they are terrible thieves. A number of knives and a hatchet were missed—they were found hidden in Myouk's sledge. We tried to prevail on Oomia to sell her long boots. To our surprise she was quite willing to part with *one*, but nothing would induce her to give up the *other*. One of the men observed her steal a knife out of the cabin and hide it in the leg of her boot. The reason was now plain. We pulled off the boot without asking leave, and found there a large assortment of articles stolen from us. Two or three knives, a spoon, a bit of hoop-iron, and a marline spike. I have tried to make them understand, by signs, that this is very wicked conduct, but they only laugh at me. They are not in the least ashamed, and evidently regard stealing as no sin.

"We have shot a musk ox. There are many of these creatures in other parts of the Arctic regions, but this is the first we have seen here. He fell to my rifle, and is now being devoured by ourselves and our dogs with great relish. He is about the size of a very small cow; has a large head and enormously thick horns, which cover the whole top of his head, bend down toward his cheeks, and then curve up and outward at the point. He is covered with long, brown hair, which almost reaches the ground, and has no tail worthy of the name. He seems to be an active and an angry creature. When I wounded him he came at me furiously, but had not pluck to charge home. As he turned away I gave him the shot that killed him. The meat is not bad, but it smells strongly of musk. Walrus is better.

"Myouk and his son Meetek and I have had a most exciting bear-hunt since we returned. I followed these men one day, as I thought them bold, active-looking fellows, who would be likely to show me good Eskimo sport. And I was not disappointed.

"About two miles from the brig we came on fresh bear tracks. A glow of the aurora gave us plenty of light. 'What is yon round white lump?' thought I. 'A bear? No, it must be a snow-wreath!' Myouk did not think so, for he ran behind a lump of ice, and became excited. He made signs to me to remain there while he and his son should go and attack the bear. They were armed each with a long lance. I must say, when I remembered the size and strength of the polar bear, that I was surprised to find these men bold enough to attack him with such arms. I had my rifle, but determined not to use it except in case of necessity. I wished to see how the natives were accustomed to act.

"They were soon ready. Gliding swiftly from one lump of ice to another, they got near enough to make a rush. I was disobedient! I followed, and when the rush was made I was not far behind them. The bear was a very large one. It uttered an angry growl on seeing the men running toward it, and rose on its hind legs to receive them. It stood nearly eight feet high when in this position, and looked really a terrible monster. I stood still behind a hummock at a distance of about fifty yards, with my rifle ready.

"On coming close up the father and son separated, and approached the bear one on each side. This divided his attention, and puzzled him very much; for, when he made a motion as if he were going to rush at Myouk, Meetek flourished his spear, and obliged him to turn—then Myouk made a demonstration, and turned him back again. Thus they were enabled to get close to its side before it could make up its mind which to attack. But the natives soon settled the question for it. Myouk was on the bear's right side, Meetek on its left. The father pricked it with the point of his lance. A tremendous roar followed, and the enraged animal turned towards him. This was just what he wanted, because it gave the son an opportunity of making a deadly thrust. Meetek was not slow to do it. He plunged his lance deep into the bear's heart, and it fell at once at full length, while a crimson stream poured out of the wound upon the snow.

"While this fight was going on I might have shot the animal through the heart with great ease, for it was quite near to me, and when it got up on its hind legs its broad chest presented a fine target. It was difficult to resist the temptation to fire, but I wished to see the native manner of doing the thing from beginning to end, so did not interfere. I was rewarded for my self-denial.

"Half an hour later, while we were dragging the carcass toward the brig, we came unexpectedly upon another bear. Myouk and Meetek at once grasped their lances and ran forward to attack him. I now resolved to play them a trick. Besides my rifle I carried a large horse-pistol in my belt. This I examined, and, finding it all right, I followed close at the heels of the Eskimos. Bruin got up on his hind legs as before, and the two men advanced close to him. I stopped when within thirty yards, cocked my rifle, and stood ready. Myouk was just going to thrust with his lance when—*bang*! went my rifle. The bear fell. It was shot right through the heart, but it struggled for some time after that. The natives seemed inclined to run away when they heard the shot, but I laughed and made signs of friendship. Then I went close up and shot the bear through the head with my pistol. This affair has filled my savage companions with deep respect for me!"

These two bears were the last they obtained that winter; but as a good supply of meat had been obtained from the Eskimos, they were relieved from anxiety for the time, and the health of the men began to improve a little. But this happy state of things did not last till spring. These sorely tried men were destined to endure much suffering before the light of the sun came back to cheer their drooping spirits.

# CHAPTER ELEVEN

## CHRISTMAS TIME—DEATH—
## RETURN OF LIGHT AND HOPE—
## DISASTERS AND FINAL DELIVERANCE

Christmas came at last, but with it came no bright sun to remind those ice-bound men of our Saviour—the "Sun of Righteousness"—whose birth the day commemorated. It was even darker than usual in Refuge Harbour on that Christmas-day. It was so dark at noon that one could not see any object more than a few yards distant from the eyes. A gale of wind from the nor'-west blew the snow-drift in whirling ghost-like clouds round the *Hope*, so that it was impossible to face it for a moment. So intense was the cold that it felt like sheets of fire being driven against the face! Truly it was a day well fitted to have depressed the heartiest of men. But man is a wonderful creature, not easy to comprehend! The very things that ought to have cast down the spirits of the men of the *Hope* were the things that helped to cheer them.

About this time, as I have said, the health of the crew had improved a little, so they were prepared to make the most of everything. Those feelings of kindliness and good-will which warm the breasts of all right-minded men at this season of the year, filled our Arctic voyagers to

R. M. Ballantyne

overflowing. Thoughts of "home" came crowding on them with a power that they had not felt at other times. Each man knew that on this day, more than any other day of that long, dark winter, the talk round a well-known hearth in Merry England would be of one who was far, far away in the dark regions of ice and snow. A tear or two that could not be forced back tumbled over rough cheeks which were not used to *that* kind of salt water; and many a silent prayer went up to call down a blessing on the heads of dear ones at home.

It blew "great guns outside," as Baker said, but what of that? it was a dead calm in the cabin! It was dark as a coal-hole on the floes. What then? it was bright as noon-day in the *Hope*! No sun blazed through the skylight, to be sure, but a lamp, filled with fat, glared on the table, and a great fire of coal glowed in the stove. Both of these together did not make the place too warm, but there were fur-coats and trousers and boots to help defy the cold. The men were few in number and not likely to see many friends on that Christmas-day. All the more reason why they should make the most of each other! Besides, they were wrong in their last idea about friends, for it chanced, on that very day, that Myouk the Eskimo paid them a visit—quite ignorant of its being Christmas, of course. Meetek was with him, and so was Oomia, and so was the baby—that remarkably fat, oily, naked baby, that seemed rather to enjoy the cold than otherwise!

They had a plum-pudding that day. Butts said it was almost as big as the head of a walrus. They had also a roast of beef—walrus-beef, of course—and first-rate it was. But before dinner the captain made them go through their usual morning work of cleaning, airing, making beds, posting journals, noting temperatures, opening the fire-hole, and redding up. For the captain was a great believer in the value of discipline. He knew that no man enjoys himself so much as he who has got through his work early—who has done his duty. It did not take them long, and when it was done the captain said, "Now, boys, we must be jolly to-day. As we can't get out we must take some exercise indoors. We shall need extra appetite to make away with that plum-pudding."

So, at it they went! Every sort of game or feat of strength known to sailors was played, or attempted. It was in the middle of all this that Myouk and his family arrived, so they were compelled to join. Even the fat baby was put into a blanket and swung round the cabin by Jim Croft, to the horror of its mother, who seemed to think it would be killed, and to the delight of its father, who didn't seem to care whether it was killed or not.

Then came the dinner. What a scene that was, to be sure! It would take a whole book to describe all that was said and done that day. The Eskimos ate till they could hardly stand—that was their usual custom. Then they lay down and went to sleep—that was their usual custom, too. The rest ate as heartily, poor fellows, as was possible for men not yet quite recovered from scurvy. They had no wine, but they had excellent coffee, and with this they drank to absent friends, sweethearts, and wives, and many other toasts, the mere mention of which raised such strong home-feelings in their breasts that some of them almost choked in the attempt to cheer. Then came songs and stories—all of them old, very old indeed—but they came out on this occasion as good as new. The great event of the evening, however, was a fancy ball, in which our friends Butts, Baker, Gregory, and Pepper distinguished themselves. They had a fiddle, and Dawkins the steward could play it. He knew nothing but Scotch reels; but what could have been better? They could all dance, or, if they

R. M. Ballantyne

could not, they all tried. Myouk and Meetek were made to join and they capered as gracefully as polar bears, which animals they strongly resembled in their hairy garments. Late in the evening came supper. It was just a repetition of dinner, with the remains of the pudding fried in bear's grease.

Thus passed Christmas-Day; much in the same way passed New Year's Day. Then the men settled down to their old style of life; but the time hung so heavy on their hands that their spirits began to sink again. The long darkness became intolerable and the fresh meat began to fail. Everything with life seemed to have forsaken the place. The captain made another trip to the Eskimo village and found the huts empty—the whole race had flown, he knew not whither! The private theatricals were at first very successful; but by degrees they lost their interest and were given up. Then a school was started and Gregory became head master. Writing and arithmetic were the only branches taught. Some of the men were much in need of instruction, and all of them took to the school with energy and much delight. It lasted longer than the theatricals did. As time wore on the fresh meat was finished, scurvy became worse; and it was as much as the men who were not quite knocked down could do to attend to those who were. Day after day Tom and Gregory and Sam Baker went out to hunt, and each day returned empty-handed. Sometimes an Arctic hare or a fox was got; but not often. At last rats were eaten as food. These creatures swarmed in the hold of the brig. They were caught in traps and shot with a bow and a blunt-headed arrow. But few of the men would eat them. The captain urged them to do so in vain. Those who did eat kept in better health than those who did not.

At last death came. Mr Mansell sank beneath the terrible

disease and was buried on the island. No grave could be dug in that hard frozen soil. The burial service was read by his sorrowing comrades over his body, which was frozen quite hard before they reached the grave, and then they laid it in a tomb of ice.

Time hung heavier than ever after that. Death is at all time a terrible visitant, but in such a place and under such circumstances it was tenfold more awful than usual. The blank in so small a band was a great one. It would perhaps have depressed them more than it did had their own situation been less desperate. But they had too fierce a battle to fight with disease, and the midnight gloom, and the bitter frost, to give way to much feeling about him who was gone.

Thus the long winter passed heavily away.

The sun came back at last, and when he came his beams shone upon a pale, shattered, and heart-weary band of men. But with his cheering light came also *hope*, and health soon followed in his train. Let young Gregory's journal tell the rest of our story, little of which now remains to be told.

"*February 21st.*—I have to record, with joy and gratitude, that the sun shone on the peaks of the ice-bergs to-day. The first time it has done so since October last. By the end of this month we shall have his rays on deck. I climbed to the top of a berg and actually bathed in sunshine this forenoon! We are all quite excited by the event, some of us even look jolly. Ah! what miserable faces my comrades have! so pale, so thin! We are all as weak as water. The captain and I are the strongest. Baker is also pretty well. Crofts and Davis are almost useless, the rest being quite helpless. The captain cooks, Baker

R. M. Ballantyne

and I hunt, Crofts and Davis attend to the sick. Another month of darkness would have killed the half of us."

"*March 10th.*—I shot a bear to-day. It did my heart good to see the faces of the men when I brought them the news and a piece of the flesh! The cold is not quite so intense now. Our coldest day this year has been the 17th of January. The glass stood at 67 degrees below zero on that morning. What a winter we have had! I shudder when I think of it. But there is more cause to be anxious about what yet lies before us. A single bear will not last long. Many weeks must pass before we are free. In June we hope to be released from our ice-prison. Fresh meat we shall then have in abundance. With it strength will return, and then, if God permits, we shall attempt to continue our voyage northward. The captain is confident on the point of open water round the Pole. The men are game for anything in spite of their sad condition."

Thus wrote Gregory at that date. Many weeks later we find him writing as follows:

"*June 15th.*—Free at last! The ice has been breaking up out at sea for some time past. It gave way in Refuge Harbour yesterday, and we warped out in the night. Everything is ready to push north again. We have been feeding heartily for many weeks on walrus, seals, wild-fowl, and last, but not least, on some grasses which make bad greens, but they have put scurvy to flight. All the men are well and strong and fit for hard work—though nothing like what they were when we first came here. Could it be otherwise? There are some of us who will carry the marks of this winter to our graves. The bright beautiful sunshine shines now, all day and all night, cheering our hearts and inspiring hope."

"*June 16th.*—All is lost! How little we know what a day may bring forth! Our good little brig is gone, and we are here on the ice without a thing in the world except the clothes on our backs. I have saved my note-book, which chanced to be in my breast-pocket when the nip took place. How awfully sudden it was! We now appreciate the wise forethought of Captain Harvey in sending the large boat to Forlorn-Hope Bay. This boat is our last and only hope. We shall have to walk forty miles before we reach it."

"Our brig went down at three o'clock this afternoon. We had warped out into the floes to catch a light breeze that was blowing outside. For some time we held on steadily to the northward, but had not got out of sight of our winter quarters when a stream of ice set down upon us and closed in all around. At first we thought nothing of this, having escaped so many dangers of the kind last autumn, but by degrees the pressure increased alarmingly. We were jammed against a great ice-field which was still fast to the shore. In a few moments the sides of our little vessel began to creak and groan loudly. The men laboured like tigers at the ice-poles, but in vain. We heard a loud report in the cabin. No one knows what it was, but I suppose it must have been the breaking of a large bolt. At any rate it was followed by a series of crashes and reports that left no doubt in our minds as to what was going on. The ice was cracking the brig as if she had been a nut-shell. 'Save yourselves, lads!' cried the captain. One or two of the men made a rush to the hatchway, intending to run below and save some of their things. I ran to the cabin-ladder in the hope of saving our log-book and journals, but we all started back in horror, for the deck at that moment burst open almost under our feet. I cast one glance down through the opening into the hold. That glance was sufficient. The massive timbers and beams

R. M. Ballantyne

were being crushed together, doubled up, split, and shivered, as if they had been rotten straws! In another moment I was on the ice, where the whole crew were assembled, looking on at the work of destruction in solemn silence.

"After bursting in the vessel's sides the ice eased off, and she at once began to settle down. We could hear the water rushing furiously into the hold. Ten minutes later she was gone! Thus end our hopes of farther discovery, and we are now left to fight our way in an open boat to the settlements on the south coast of Greenland. We have little time to think. Prompt action must be our watchword now, if we would escape from this world of ice.

"*July 20th.*—I have not entered a line in this journal since our vessel was lost  Our work has been so severe, and our sufferings so great, that I have had no heart for writing. Our walk to the place where we left the boat was a hard one, but we were cheered by finding the boat all safe, and the provisions and stores just as we left them. There was not enough to last out the voyage, but we had guns and powder. It is in vain to attempt to describe the events of the last few weeks. Constant, and hard, and cold work—at the oars, with the ice-poles—warping, hauling, and shoving. Beset by ice; driving before storms; detained by thick fogs; often wet to the skin; always tired, almost starving—such has been our fate since that sad day when our brig went down. And yet I don't think there is one of our party who would not turn about on the spot and renew our voyage of discovery, if he only got a chance of going in a well-appointed vessel. As it is, we must push on. Home! home! is our cry now."

"*August 1st.*—We are now in clover, after having been reduced to think of roasting our shoes for breakfast. For three days last week we ate nothing at all. Our powder has been expended for some weeks past. On Monday we finished our last morsel of the gull that Pepper managed to bring down with a stone. Tuesday was a terrible day. The agony of hunger was worse than I had expected it to be. Nevertheless, we tried hard to cheer each other as we laboured at the oars. Our only hope was to fall in with natives. Signs of them were seen everywhere, and we expected to hear their shouts at every point of land we doubled. The captain suggested that we should try *shoe-soup* on Wednesday morning! He was more than half in earnest, but spoke as if he were jesting. Pepper cocked his ears as if there was some hope still of work for him to do in his own line. Jim Crofts pulled off his shoe, and, looking at it earnestly, wondered if the sole would make a very tough chop. We all laughed, but I cannot say that the laugh sounded hearty. On the Thursday I began to feel weak, but the pangs of hunger were not so bad. Our eyes seemed very large and wolfish. I could not help shuddering when I thought of the terrible things that men have done when reduced to this state."

"That evening, as we rounded a point, we saw an Eskimo boy high on a cliff, with a net in his hand. He did not see us for some time, and we were so excited that we stopped rowing to watch him in breathless silence. Thousands of birds were flying round his head among the cliffs. How often we had tried to kill some of these with sticks and stones, in vain! The net he held was a round one, with a long handle. Suddenly he made a dashing sweep with it and caught two of the birds as they passed! We now saw that a number of dead birds lay at his feet. In one moment our boat was ashore and we scrambled up the cliffs in eager haste. The boy fled in terror, but before he was well out of sight every man was seated on a ledge of rock with a bird at his mouth, sucking the blood! Hunger like ours

R. M. Ballantyne

despises cookery! It was fortunate that there were not many birds, else we should have done ourselves harm by eating too much. I have eaten many a good meal in my life, but never one so sweet, or for which I was so thankful, as that meal of raw birds, devoured on the cliffs of Greenland!

"That night we reached the Eskimo village, where we now lie. We find that it is only two days' journey from this place to the Danish settlements. There we mean to get on board the first ship that is bound for Europe—no matter what port she sails for. Meanwhile we rest our weary limbs in peace, for our dangers are past, and—thanks be to God—we are saved."

---

Reader, my tale is told. A little book cannot be made to contain a long story, else would I have narrated many more of the strange and interesting events that befell our adventurers during that voyage. But enough has been written to give some idea of what is done and suffered by those daring men who attempt to navigate the Polar seas.

THE END

# Other books by this author

Black Ivory

Red Rooney

The Coral Island

The Golden Dream

The Hot Swamp

The Island Queen

The Red Eric

Chasing The Sun

Sunk at Sea

The Battle and the Breeze

The Lively Poll

R. M. Ballantyne

# Choose from Thousands of 1stWorldLibrary Classics By

A. M. Barnard
Ada Leverson
Adolphus William Ward
Aesop
Agatha Christie
Alexander Aaronsohn
Alexander Kielland
Alexandre Dumas
Alfred Gatty
Alfred Ollivant
Alice Duer Miller
Alice Turner Curtis
Alice Dunbar
Allen Chapman
Alleyne Ireland
Ambrose Bierce
Amelia E. Barr
Amory H. Bradford
Andrew Lang
Andrew McFarland Davis
Andy Adams
Angela Brazil
Anna Alice Chapin
Anna Sewell
Annie Besant
Annie Hamilton Donnell
Annie Payson Call
Annie Roe Carr
Annonaymous
Anton Chekhov
Archibald Lee Fletcher
Arnold Bennett
Arthur C. Benson
Arthur Conan Doyle
Arthur M. Winfield
Arthur Ransome
Arthur Schnitzler
Arthur Train
Atticus
B.H. Baden-Powell
B. M. Bower
B. C. Chatterjee
Baroness Emmuska Orczy
Baroness Orczy
Basil King
Bayard Taylor
Ben Macomber
Bertha Muzzy Bower
Bjornstjerne Bjornson

Booth Tarkington
Boyd Cable
Bram Stoker
C. Collodi
C. E. Orr
C. M. Ingleby
Carolyn Wells
Catherine Parr Traill
Charles A. Eastman
Charles Amory Beach
Charles Dickens
Charles Dudley Warner
Charles Farrar Browne
Charles Ives
Charles Kingsley
Charles Klein
Charles Hanson Towne
Charles Lathrop Pack
Charles Romyn Dake
Charles Whibley
Charles Willing Beale
Charlotte M. Braeme
Charlotte M. Yonge
Charlotte Perkins Stetson
Clair W. Hayes
Clarence Day Jr.
Clarence E. Mulford
Clemence Housman
Confucius
Coningsby Dawson
Cornelis DeWitt Wilcox
Cyril Burleigh
D. H. Lawrence
Daniel Defoe
David Garnett
Dinah Craik
Don Carlos Janes
Donald Keyhoe
Dorothy Kilner
Dougan Clark
Douglas Fairbanks
E. Nesbit
E. P. Roe
E. Phillips Oppenheim
E. S. Brooks
Earl Barnes
Edgar Rice Burroughs
Edith Van Dyne
Edith Wharton

Edward Everett Hale
Edward J. O'Biren
Edward S. Ellis
Edwin L. Arnold
Eleanor Atkins
Eleanor Hallowell Abbott
Eliot Gregory
Elizabeth Gaskell
Elizabeth McCracken
Elizabeth Von Arnim
Ellem Key
Emerson Hough
Emilie F. Carlen
Emily Bronte
Emily Dickinson
Enid Bagnold
Enilor Macartney Lane
Erasmus W. Jones
Ernie Howard Pie
Ethel May Dell
Ethel Turner
Ethel Watts Mumford
Eugene Sue
Eugenie Foa
Eugene Wood
Eustace Hale Ball
Evelyn Everett-green
Everard Cotes
F. H. Cheley
F. J. Cross
F. Marion Crawford
Fannie E. Newberry
Federick Austin Ogg
Ferdinand Ossendowski
Fergus Hume
Florence A. Kilpatrick
Fremont B. Deering
Francis Bacon
Francis Darwin
Frances Hodgson Burnett
Frances Parkinson Keyes
Frank Gee Patchin
Frank Harris
Frank Jewett Mather
Frank L. Packard
Frank V. Webster
Frederic Stewart Isham
Frederick Trevor Hill
Frederick Winslow Taylor

Friedrich Kerst
Friedrich Nietzsche
Fyodor Dostoyevsky
G.A. Henty
G.K. Chesterton
Gabrielle E. Jackson
Garrett P. Serviss
Gaston Leroux
George A. Warren
George Ade
Geroge Bernard Shaw
George Cary Eggleston
George Durston
George Ebers
George Eliot
George Gissing
George MacDonald
George Meredith
George Orwell
George Sylvester Viereck
George Tucker
George W. Cable
George Wharton James
Gertrude Atherton
Gordon Casserly
Grace E. King
Grace Gallatin
Grace Greenwood
Grant Allen
Guillermo A. Sherwell
Gulielma Zollinger
Gustav Flaubert
H. A. Cody
H. B. Irving
H. C. Bailey
H. G. Wells
H. H. Munro
H. Irving Hancock
H. R. Naylor
H. Rider Haggard
H. W. C. Davis
Haldeman Julius
Hall Caine
Hamilton Wright Mabie
Hans Christian Andersen
Harold Avery
Harold McGrath
Harriet Beecher Stowe
Harry Castlemon
Harry Coghill
Harry Houidini

Hayden Carruth
Helent Hunt Jackson
Helen Nicolay
Hendrik Conscience
Hendy David Thoreau
Henri Barbusse
Henrik Ibsen
Henry Adams
Henry Ford
Henry Frost
Henry James
Henry Jones Ford
Henry Seton Merriman
Henry W Longfellow
Herbert A. Giles
Herbert Carter
Herbert N. Casson
Herman Hesse
Hildegard G. Frey
Homer
Honore De Balzac
Horace B. Day
Horace Walpole
Horatio Alger Jr.
Howard Pyle
Howard R. Garis
Hugh Lofting
Hugh Walpole
Humphry Ward
Ian Maclaren
Inez Haynes Gillmore
Irving Bacheller
Isabel Cecilia Williams
Isabel Hornibrook
Israel Abrahams
Ivan Turgenev
J. G.Austin
J. Henri Fabre
J. M. Barrie
J. M. Walsh
J. Macdonald Oxley
J. R. Miller
J. S. Fletcher
J. S. Knowles
J. Storer Clouston
J. W. Duffield
Jack London
Jacob Abbott
James Allen
James Andrews
James Baldwin

James Branch Cabell
James DeMille
James Joyce
James Lane Allen
James Lane Allen
James Oliver Curwood
James Oppenheim
James Otis
James R. Driscoll
Jane Abbott
Jane Austen
Jane L. Stewart
Janet Aldridge
Jens Peter Jacobsen
Jerome K. Jerome
Jessie Graham Flower
John Buchan
John Burroughs
John Cournos
John F. Kennedy
John Gay
John Glasworthy
John Habberton
John Joy Bell
John Kendrick Bangs
John Milton
John Philip Sousa
John Taintor Foote
Jonas Lauritz Idemil Lie
Jonathan Swift
Joseph A. Altsheler
Joseph Carey
Joseph Conrad
Joseph E. Badger Jr
Joseph Hergesheimer
Joseph Jacobs
Jules Vernes
Julian Hawthrone
Julie A Lippmann
Justin Huntly McCarthy
Kakuzo Okakura
Karle Wilson Baker
Kate Chopin
Kenneth Grahame
Kenneth McGaffey
Kate Langley Bosher
Kate Langley Bosher
Katherine Cecil Thurston
Katherine Stokes
L. A. Abbot
L. T. Meade

L. Frank Baum
Latta Griswold
Laura Dent Crane
Laura Lee Hope
Laurence Housman
Lawrence Beasley
Leo Tolstoy
Leonid Andreyev
Lewis Carroll
Lewis Sperry Chafer
Lilian Bell
Lloyd Osbourne
Louis Hughes
Louis Joseph Vance
Louis Tracy
Louisa May Alcott
Lucy Fitch Perkins
Lucy Maud Montgomery
Luther Benson
Lydia Miller Middleton
Lyndon Orr
M. Corvus
M. H. Adams
Margaret E. Sangster
Margret Howth
Margaret Vandercook
Margaret W. Hungerford
Margret Penrose
Maria Edgeworth
Maria Thompson Daviess
Mariano Azuela
Marion Polk Angellotti
Mark Overton
Mark Twain
Mary Austin
Mary Cole
Mary Hastings Bradley
Mary Roberts Rinehart
Mary Rowlandson
M. Wollstonecraft Shelley
Maud Lindsay
Max Beerbohm
Myra Kelly
Nathaniel Hawthrone
Nicolo Machiavelli
O. F. Walton
Oscar Wilde
Owen Johnson
P.G. Wodehouse
Paul and Mabel Thorne

Paul G. Tomlinson
Paul Severing
Percy Brebner
Percy Keese Fitzhugh
Peter B. Kyne
Plato
Quincy Allen
R. Derby Holmes
R. L. Stevenson
R. S. Ball
Rabindranath Tagore
Rahul Alvares
Ralph Bonehill
Ralph Henry Barbour
Ralph Victor
Ralph Waldo Emmerson
Rene Descartes
Ray Cummings
Rex Beach
Rex E. Beach
Richard Harding Davis
Richard Jefferies
Richard Le Gallienne
Robert Barr
Robert Frost
Robert Gordon Anderson
Robert L. Drake
Robert Lansing
Robert Lynd
Robert Michael Ballantyne
Robert W. Chambers
Rosa Nouchette Carey
Rudyard Kipling
Saint Augustine
Samuel B. Allison
Samuel Hopkins Adams
Sarah Bernhardt
Sarah C. Hallowell
Selma Lagerlof
Sherwood Anderson
Sigmund Freud
Standish O'Grady
Stanley Weyman
Stella Benson
Stella M. Francis
Stephen Crane
Stewart Edward White
Stijn Streuvels
Swami Abhedananda
Swami Parmananda
T. S. Ackland

T. S. Arthur
The Princess Der Ling
Thomas A. Janvier
Thomas A Kempis
Thomas Anderton
Thomas Bailey Aldrich
Thomas Bulfinch
Thomas De Quincey
Thomas Dixon
Thomas H. Huxley
Thomas Hardy
Thomas More
Thornton W. Burgess
U. S. Grant
Upton Sinclair
Valentine Williams
Various Authors
Vaughan Kester
Victor Appleton
Victor G. Durham
Victoria Cross
Virginia Woolf
Wadsworth Camp
Walter Camp
Walter Scott
Washington Irving
Wilbur Lawton
Wilkie Collins
Willa Cather
Willard F. Baker
William Dean Howells
William le Queux
W. Makepeace Thackeray
William W. Walter
William Shakespeare
Winston Churchill
Yei Theodora Ozaki
Yogi Ramacharaka
Young E. Allison
Zane Grey

www.ingramcontent.com/pod-product-compliance
Lightning Source LLC
Chambersburg PA
CBHW031851170626
46807CB00004B/1678